It's Not About You

It's Not About You

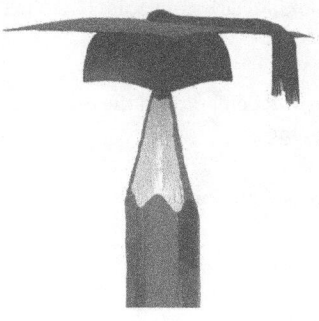

INSIDER STRATEGIES FOR ELITE MBA APPLICANTS

Barbara J. Coward

MBA ADMISSIONS CONSULTANT & CAREER STRATEGIST

 | Books

Published by Advantage Books, Charleston, South Carolina.
An imprint of Advantage Media.

ADVANTAGE is a registered trademark, and the Advantage colophon is a trademark of Advantage Media Group, Inc.

Printed in the United States of America.

10 9 8 7 6 5 4 3 2 1

ISBN: 979-8-89188-326-0 (Paperback)
ISBN: 979-8-89188-375-8 (eBook)

Library of Congress Control Number: 2025927340

Cover and layout design by Ruthie Wood.

This publication is designed to provide accurate and authoritative information in regard to the subject matter covered. It is sold with the understanding that the publisher is not engaged in rendering legal, accounting, or other professional services. If legal advice or other expert assistance is required, the services of a competent professional person should be sought.

Advantage Books is an imprint of Advantage Media Group. Advantage Media helps busy entrepreneurs, CEOs, and leaders write and publish a book to grow their business and become the authority in their field. Advantage authors comprise an exclusive community of industry professionals, idea-makers, and thought leaders. For more information go to **advantagemedia.com**.

For Michael McCarthy, the finest boss and mentor of my career, with deepest gratitude.

With Mike in the early 1990s when I received an achievement award at American Express in Boston

CONTENTS

INTRODUCTION 1
Welcome to the Real World of MBA Admissions

PART I 15
Understanding Today's MBA Admissions Landscape

    CHAPTER 1 17
    Business School Admissions: A Reality Check

    CHAPTER 2 43
    The Stakeholder Web

    CHAPTER 3 63
    How Decisions Really Get Made

PART II 75
The Art and Science of Standing Out

    CHAPTER 4 77
    Position Yourself for Success

CHAPTER 5 99
Your Application Strategy

CHAPTER 6 131
The Psychology of Applications

PART III 145
Mastering the Process

CHAPTER 7 147
The Power Shift

CHAPTER 8 167
Making the Most of Your MBA Experience

CONCLUSION 193

ACKNOWLEDGMENTS 199

ABOUT THE AUTHOR 201

INTRODUCTION

Welcome to the Real World
of MBA Admissions

The story was one I'd heard countless times. Riley had dreamed of applying to an MBA program for several years, but a rough college semester that hurt his GPA had him worried his stats wouldn't measure up. It didn't help that others told him, "There's no way you'll get into a good program." When he contacted me, he expected to hear more of the same and was surprised when I suggested that his chances might be better than he thought. He shared his story with me, and together, we uncovered the unique and compelling aspects of his journey, especially his resilience, clarity around professional goals, and evidence of leadership acumen. Recognizing that he was so much more than his transcript gave Riley the confidence to share his story persuasively and in his own powerful voice across all aspects of his application, from his résumé to essays to interviews. He ended up at a top ten school!

Riley is like so many clients I work with who are frozen by self-doubt and can benefit from support as they navigate the complex landscape of MBA admissions. I have written *It's Not About You* because I've seen how hard it can be just to start the process, how confusing it can be to apply to programs and decide among offers, and how demoralizing rejections often are.

Some get so overwhelmed they start to rethink if they should get an MBA in the first place. Or if they do decide to pursue one, where in the world (sometimes literally) should they apply? What are their chances? Should they aim for only a top-tier program, or is that too risky? If they do reach the point of narrowing down a target list, they might be stymied by the application process itself. When a disappointing GMAT score comes back, many would-be applicants give up, perhaps caving to shattered confidence, letting work demands take precedence, or questioning an MBA degree's return on investment because of a Reddit thread they happen to read.

Applying for, and gaining acceptance to, MBA programs is hard. But mostly, it can seem like a mystery. Why does one strong candidate get in but another one doesn't? And just when you think you understand what admissions committees value, the rules change. New priorities emerge, recruitment strategies evolve, and global events reshape the applicant pool. Somewhere between test scores and essays, alumni panels and networking events, the reality is that the process is far more complex than most applicants anticipate, and the emotional ups and downs can take their toll.

Why This Book; Why Now

It's Not About You fills the void where traditional advice falls short. Many applicants mistakenly believe MBA admissions rely solely on test scores and GPAs. The true nature of the process is more nuanced, involving institutional priorities, stakeholder interests, market forces, and complex relationships that often override individual achievements.

In recent years, business schools have broadened their definitions of merit to include factors such as culture fit or alignment with emerging industries. And they deploy sophisticated data analytics to manage yield rates and target underrepresented demographics.

In addition, the MBA landscape has expanded. Beyond two-year, full-time MBA programs, applicants can choose among part-time, online, executive, and specialized master's programs. Schools have also introduced deferred-admission tracks for undergraduates and accelerated formats for mid-career professionals. Decisions that were once made based on the brand prestige of a program must now factor in program structure, networking opportunities, curriculum innovation, and postgraduation outcomes.

What This Book Can Do for You

Success with MBA applications requires more than presenting your achievements; it requires understanding how decisions really get made, who and what influence them, and how to position yourself persuasively at each stage. Throughout the chapters that follow, you will:

- **See the bigger picture:** Recognize how institutional priorities and market dynamics influence each class profile.

- **Clarify your narrative:** Identify and articulate the experiences, values, and goals that differentiate you and convey your unique life story.

- **Choose strategically:** Develop a school list that balances reach, target, and safety programs while maximizing fit.

- **Navigate the process:** Master each application component, from essays and recommendations to interviews and multiple school acceptances.

- **Manage the emotional journey:** Build confidence over self-doubt, resilience in the face of rejection, momentum as the process stretches on, and clarity as you make your final choices.

The chapters of *It's Not About You* are clustered into three parts, progressing from understanding the broader context to taking action. Part I, Understanding Today's MBA Admissions Landscape, reveals current admissions criteria and the hidden factors that influence decisions. Part II, The Art and Science of Standing Out, provides concrete strategies for positioning yourself and developing your application. Finally, part III, Mastering the Process, guides you through the post-acceptance phase, including waiting lists, dealing with rejection, comparing offers, deciding where to attend, and career management.

You'll also find lots of examples throughout the book to see how the strategies I recommend work out when implemented. When I have permission to do so, or when I pull examples from the public domain, I use the real names of applicants, alumni, admissions officers, or others I cite. But in many cases, to protect the confidentiality of my clients and preserve the trust of admissions professionals who speak freely with me, I have disguised identifying details and changed names.

Throughout the book, you'll also find Pro Tips in which I highlight practical takeaways—notable advice that goes beyond the basics. Near the end of each chapter, you'll find Your Bottom Line, in which I recap the content of that chapter and its impact on applicants. Following that, each chapter closes with Your Strategic SWOT, playing on the popular strategic analysis framework for evaluating strengths, weaknesses, opportunities, and threats. "Your Strategic SWOT" consists of questions and prompts that encourage active reflection and help you apply what you're learning to your unique circumstances.

PRO TIP: UNDERSTAND THE MEANING BEHIND THE TITLE

Your credentials matter, but MBA admissions is about much more than you and your credentials alone, as you're going to learn throughout *It's Not About You*. I have seen my clients take rejection so personally (which is understandable since that is human nature). And I've seen them believe that if they can control every little thing along the admissions journey, that will make the difference between an acceptance and a rejection: *If I choose this post-MBA goal over another to talk about in my essay, I'll have an edge*, or *If I don't click with the alum in the interview, I'll lose my chances*. This faulty belief that it's all about you and all up to you causes undue pressure and stress.

My Insider Perspective

I've spent decades on both sides of the MBA admissions desk as an institutional insider and a consultant guiding applicants around the globe. From launching one of the UK's first professional MBA admissions offices to advising elite schools worldwide, I've gained a deep understanding of how programs operate and what influences admissions decisions. Through my firm, MBA 360° Admissions, I've helped clients earn offers from schools such as Harvard Business School (HBS), Stanford Graduate School of Business, and the Wharton School of the University of Pennsylvania (Wharton), as well as find great-fit options beyond the top tier. I also draw on conversations with prominent business leaders, political figures, and media personalities I've met over the course of my career to inform the guidance I offer in this book. I'm continuously fascinated by how people advance in their careers and achieve success at the top of their industries.

My goal is to use all this experience to narrow the distance between applicants and admissions decision-makers to show you what really matters. When I work with a client, I want to help the admissions committee envision that applicant as a member of the cohort, contributing to the learning in their classrooms, enriching campus life, and being an engaged alum after graduation. This is essentially about bridging the business school's world and the applicant's world to reduce that distance.

WHY I WROTE THIS BOOK

A pivotal moment in my own career came when I was working in the mutual fund industry in Boston. I was in my mid-twenties and had recently earned a big promotion to division controller even though I had not taken one accounting class in college. (I graduated with a decidedly nonquantitative undergraduate degree in French literature!) I reported to a Brooks Brothers–suited executive who would often recount stories from his days studying at HBS during our many mentorship meetings in his office. As part of my continued career growth, he suggested that I get a part-time MBA, since the company would sponsor it.

This was back before social media and the internet, so I relied on word of mouth to learn about programs and chose Boston College's Carroll School of Management simply because a couple of guys I dated went there. (Insert eye roll.) I was nearly one-third of the way through when I moved to rural England. At the time, my future husband couldn't leave his third-generation family business, which manufactured and sold brushes to customers around the world, including to the British Royal Family. Since I was leaving my job, my family, and my hometown, I was determined to continue my MBA and establish my own network in a foreign country. And so I did. After graduating, the dean asked me to set up my alma mater's first-ever professional MBA admissions office. This was when I started to study the MBA landscape, visiting schools such as Wharton and the University of California, Los Angeles Anderson School of Management to benchmark with top business schools back home. I brought on dedicated admissions staff, traveled the world from Tokyo to Toronto recruiting students, and made difficult admissions decisions.

Over the past thirty years, I've witnessed so many variations of the applicant journey. For instance, the husband of a close friend was admitted to the University of Chicago's Booth School of Business and Duke University's Fuqua School of Business in the early 1990s. He was leaning toward Booth, but his wife in Boston didn't want to live in another cold climate. And as a newly married couple, he (wisely) knew that he had to take her preferences into consideration.

The following year, I visited them on campus … in Durham, North Carolina!

That example stayed with me. These choices about where to apply, where to go, and how to shape your story are deeply personal, often more complex than rankings or reputation alone can capture and often involving other people in your life. What I love most today is working with prospective MBA applicants, helping them see the strategy in their own stories.

So I wrote this book to empower you, the applicant, at the stage when you do have power, even if it doesn't always feel like it. Before decisions are made and offers extended, this is your moment. Schools might seem to hold all the cards, but they're also trying to win *you*.

IF WE WERE IN SESSION TOGETHER ...

My hope is that reading this book will feel like we're sitting across from each other on Zoom, talking things through. I come to my work not to judge or push clients toward a particular path but to ask the right questions, reflect what they may have forgotten that is valuable about themselves, and help them move forward with clarity and confidence.

I want this book to be your guide, not only for strategy but for support, because this process isn't just about selecting schools and crafting essays. It's about navigating uncertainty, managing stress, and staying connected with what really matters. The process is emotionally demanding, and you deserve someone in your corner who can hold space for all of it.

> Sam Shiah is the founder of Wall Street Mastermind and coaches clients considering investment banking careers. In one of our conversations, he described his role with clients this way: "I raise the floor to a higher level for them." I love that description! That's exactly what I do with my MBA admissions clients and now do for you in this book.

WHO THIS BOOK IS FOR

It's Not About You is for anyone seeking expert guidance and an insider's perspective on the complex journey to acceptance at top-tier MBA programs.

This book is for you if you fall into the following category of the traditional MBA applicant:

- aged twenty-five to thirty-five

- three to seven years of professional experience, likely in consulting, finance, or tech

- motivated, ambitious, and ready to invest significant time and effort in your MBA journey

- seeking professional growth and advancement, or a career transition, or simply new challenges

It's Not About You is also for those outside of the traditional applicant pool.

- early-career professionals younger than age twenty-five with less than a few years of work experience, beginning to explore the MBA path, including those considering deferred-admission programs

- mid-career or even advanced professionals looking to pivot or grow even further in their careers but perhaps also needing to weave MBA studies into their existing lives and not the other way around

- applicants from less conventional paths (personal and/or professional) wondering if they'll be a competitive candidate

Or maybe you're not even a prospective applicant at all. Perhaps you see yourself in one of these categories:

- career counselors and coaches, undergraduate advisors, and others who guide students toward graduate business education

- HR professionals and corporate talent development teams that sponsor employees seeking MBAs

- parents and family members supporting MBA candidates, especially those making significant financial investments

- business school staff and administrators interested in how applicants experience and interpret the admissions process

- media covering stories about the MBA admissions space and publishing program rankings.

While this book's core mission is to support applicants, its insights into institutional dynamics, decision-making, and applicant strategy will be useful to anyone engaged in the broader world of MBA admissions.

ABOUT *ELITE*

The word *elite* appears in the subtitle of this book—*Insider Strategies for Elite MBA Applicants*—but *elite MBA* might not mean what you think it does, at least not as I am defining it. In common usage, *elite* refers to the Magnificent Seven or M7 business schools at Chicago, Columbia, Harvard, Massachusetts Institute of Technology, Northwestern, Stanford, and Wharton. These programs are the most selective, well funded, and globally recognized. They have the resources to attract top faculty, host marquee recruiters, and offer extensive alumni networks. They are exceptional institutions.

But for this book, *elite* is defined more broadly. *It's Not About You* does focus on the more competitive end of the MBA landscape, but it rejects—while still respecting—a narrow, rankings- or brand-obsessed definition of *elite*. The list of top-tier programs I want to help you consider and apply to goes well beyond the limited list that's often referred to as the top ten (inclusive of the M7) or the top twenty.

 PRO TIP: DEFINE *ELITE MBA* ON YOUR OWN TERMS

There are plenty of schools that don't carry the most prestigious brand name but might offer the right academic fit, culture, or career opportunities for you, making them *elite* for you. Many excellent candidates turn down top ten offers to attend schools that better align with their personal or professional values, goals, and needs. In other words, they define *elite* on their own terms.

For example, I recently saw a job posting on LinkedIn that included a "distinguished MBA" in the list of qualifications sought. It made me pause. Are they using *distinguished* as a synonym for *elite* and seeking graduates of an M7 or top ten MBA program? The same thing happened with a job description that mentioned "leading MBA." Their definitions of *distinguished* or *leading* might not be the same as yours or mine. But the point here is that terminology can be confusing, and I encourage you not to get too caught up in it but instead to focus on what you want out of an MBA and how to position yourself for the best program for you.

WHAT DIFFERENTIATES THIS BOOK

It's important to note that this is not a fill-in-the-blank workbook or a tactical how-to guide on every step of the MBA application process. You won't find detailed instructions on formatting your résumé or step-by-step essay templates. (I'll recommend resources you can turn to for those sorts of needs.) Instead, this book offers high-level strategic guidance, real-life examples, and hard-earned insights—the kind of advice you would struggle to find among the information overload of online tips and opinions.

What sets this book apart from many other admissions coaching resources is that I address the psychological aspects of the process so that you can be a more confident, resilient MBA candidate. (One of my clients who worked at Citi Treasury Investments in NYC said working with me was like having a therapist!) I also cover complex organizational behavior dynamics in higher education to equip you with a macro level of knowledge most applicants are not privy to. These often-overlooked perspectives deepen your understanding of how elite admissions really work and empower you to make thoughtful, informed decisions that align with your goals.

Power in the Process

In the end, understanding that *it's not about you* is paradoxically what gives you your best chance of success. While MBA admissions can feel intensely personal, understanding the institutional perspective behind decisions is what empowers you and enables you to find, and gain acceptance to, the program you will thrive in.

I may not know each of you personally, but I know there is value in your life story. I know you have something to offer the right MBA program for you. I am committed to sharing my knowledge so you understand the realities of MBA admissions and the best strategies for positioning yourself within those realities so that your story can be heard.

It's Not About You is rooted in the idea that the MBA application journey is not only strategic but also human. You're not just applying to business school; you're choosing a chapter of your life.

Thank you for reading this book and for letting me play a small part in your professional and personal journey. Now, let's get to work!

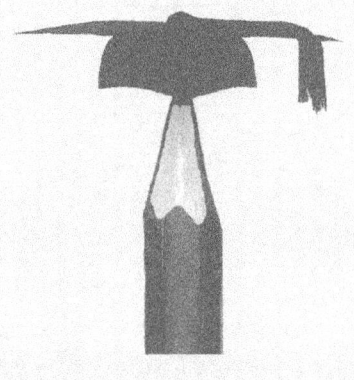

PART I

Understanding Today's MBA Admissions Landscape

CHAPTER 1

Business School Admissions: A Reality Check

I have good news and bad news. Let's start with the good: You have more information at your fingertips than ever about MBA admissions. Doors are open to more types of applicants than ever. And applicants are being evaluated more as whole people, not just grades and test scores. The bad news? *More* information doesn't always bring clarity. *More* types of applicants means more competition. And *more* holistic evaluation can make it confusing when the time comes to tell your story in applications and interviews. The current admissions landscape may be transparent and forgiving, but it is also filled with a lot of *mores*, making the competition and potential for feeling overwhelmed greater than ever.

MBA Admissions in Simpler Times

To understand current dynamics, it's helpful to look at the past. Harvard Business School's (HBS) MBA program began in 1908 with invitation-only admissions and the first cohort of eighty men.[1] In contrast, only 9 percent of 9,856 applicants were admitted to HBS for the class of 2026.[2] At Stanford, the MBA class of 2026 earned their spots through an acceptance rate of just 5.8 percent,[3] a far cry from the experience of the two men first awarded MBAs at Stanford in 1927.[4]

Since those early days, MBA programs have proliferated, with more than thirteen thousand schools worldwide offering management degrees, and candidate demand has surged. Applications to graduate business programs rose 12 percent globally from 2023 to 2024, and the most prestigious programs remain fiercely selective, requiring applicants to distinguish themselves with their personal and professional stories.[5]

---

1   "History," About, Harvard Business School, https://www.hbs.edu/about/history.

2   Marc Ethier, "MBA Class of 2026: At Harvard, a Massive Rebound in MBA Applications," *Poets & Quants*, September 23, 2024, https://poetsandquants.com/2024/09/23/mba-class-of-2026-at-harvard-a-massive-rebound-in-mba-applications/.

3   Marc Ethier, "Stanford MBA Class of 2026: Apps Up but GSB's Diversity Takes a Hit," *Poets & Quants*, October 15, 2024, https://poetsandquants.com/2024/10/15/mba-class-of-2026-apps-up-but-stanford-gsbs-diversity-takes-a-hit/.

4   "Our History," Stanford Graduate School of Business, https://www.gsb.stanford.edu/experience/news-history/history.

5   Laura Spitalniak, "Applications Spike for MBAs in 2024–25, Study Says," *Higher Ed Dive*, October 28, 2024, https://www.highereddive.com/news/mba-applications-spike-2024-2025-gmac-business-graduate/731132/; and Andrew Walker, "Four Unexpected Findings from GMAC's 2024 Business School Application Trends Survey," *EFMD Global*, November 7, 2024, https://blog.efmdglobal.org/2024/11/07/four-unexpected-findings-from-gmacs-2024-business-school-application-trends-survey/.

The M7 MBA Programs

Chicago Booth School of Business (University of Chicago)

Columbia Business School (Columbia University)

Harvard Business School (Harvard University)

Kellogg School of Management (Northwestern University)

MIT Sloan School of Management (Massachusetts Institute of Technology)

Stanford Graduate School of Business (Stanford University)

Wharton School (University of Pennsylvania)

The Power of Context

"Why should I care about these historical shifts?" you might ask. After all, you want to pursue an MBA now or in the near future, not in 1927! Knowing how the landscape has changed matters because acceptance into the MBA program of your dreams requires understanding the realities of today's admissions scene.[6] Your grandpa's Wharton MBA from decades ago or your mom's from the 1990s gives their advice some credence as they support you in your admissions process. But unless they are actively involved in MBA admissions today, they are, understandably, not likely to be up on the latest ins and outs. With my unique perspective from having worked both sides of the desk as an MBA admissions officer and MBA admissions consultant, I can help you understand the rules of the game today.

---

6   Spitalniak, "Applications Spike for MBAs."

Today's MBA admissions landscape demonstrates three key characteristics: transparency, agility, and strategic thinking.

- Power dynamics in MBA admissions have shifted in candidates' favor because the process is more **transparent** than ever, thanks to technology and new media sources that equip you with knowledge and insights to both inform your strategy and help minimize stress and worry.

- Recruiting practices and decisions are highly **agile**, as schools react to, and capitalize on, macro factors related to public policy, public health, societal trends, industry developments such as mass layoffs, mobility, and more.

- Business schools are more **strategic** than ever. They are taking a more holistic look at candidates (not just grades, test scores, and career trajectory) to reflect their mission-driven priorities, and they are considering their own financial bottom lines.

> Today's MBA admissions landscape demonstrates three key characteristics: transparency, agility, and strategic thinking.

Understanding these realities provides critical context for your own strategic decisions about where to apply, when to apply, how to craft your application, and which offer to accept. And this context helps you understand that it's not about you. Let's take a closer look at these three factors.

Information: The Double-Edged Sword

Admissions offices operate in a highly visible, highly scrutinized environment. The rise of social media has brought a new level of public accountability to schools' decisions. For much of the MBA's history, the admissions process was opaque and one-sided. You'd submit your application into a black hole and hope for the best. But that's no longer the reality. Thanks to technology, social media, and applicant-driven content, you now have access to a wealth of information that once lived behind closed doors.

That's both a blessing and a curse—for applicants and programs. As an applicant, you don't have to rely only on a program's own marketing materials, but you might find yourself overwhelmed by all the other sources at your fingertips. Admissions offices benefit by having so many avenues for publicizing their programs but can't always control the narrative when social media takes on a life of its own.

THE ECOSYSTEM OF MBA ADMISSIONS ADVICE

Thanks to this age of accountability, real-time admissions data is now publicly available. You can see real-time updates on interview invites and acceptance waves (anonymously, of course), as well as read about applicant success stories and get advice on digital channels, such as Clear Admit's MBA LiveWire and forums such as GMAT Club and Reddit's r/MBA. For personalized guidance, independent MBA admissions consultants can be a valuable resource. Let's look at these sources and more.

Online MBA Admissions Insights

There are many online resources for everything, from application strategy advice to interview practice drills and live, interactive data on admissions decisions and timing. Examples include the following:

- **School-run content:** Official blogs, virtual Q&A sessions, and sample essays are found on program websites, such as HBS's *MBA Voices Blog,* Stanford Graduate School of Business's (Stanford GSB) *Insights* blog, and Inbox Application Insights email series from the assistant dean for admissions at Yale School of Management (Yale SOM).

- **Industry newsletters:** *Poets & Quants*, the Graduate Management Admission Council's (GMAC) *BusinessBecause*, and Clear Admit are go-to sources for keeping abreast of trends, acceptances, and yield data. (See figure 1 for a visual from Clear Admit.)

- **Online forums and communities:** Reddit's r/MBA and the GMAT Club forum are popular for real-time chatter and peer intel, but be aware they can be filled with contradictory advice from all the commentators.

- **Webinars and podcasts:** Live and on-demand sessions from MBA.com (GMAC), Accepted Admissions, and *The GMAT Club Podcast* offer expert panels, school deep-dives, and Q&A with insiders.

- **Test prep blogs and platforms:** Magoosh and Manhattan Prep's GMAT blog publish strategy articles, practice drills, and video tutorials, often behind a low-cost subscription. There are numerous test prep coaching services that publish helpful content on their websites, such as City Test Prep and Dominate Test Prep.

- **Social media:** LinkedIn posts from admissions directors and Instagram "day in the life" takeovers by current students provide behind-the-scenes glimpses.

- **Independent MBA admissions consultant content:** Some of my peer consultants, such as Personal MBA Coach and Stacey

Blackman, offer advice through YouTube channels and blogs. I also publish blogs with admissions tips on my website.

- **Innovative consulting services:** Popular services such as ApplicantLab package prerecorded workshops, score feedback, and essay reviews at a fraction of traditional consulting rates.

I have chosen to list only the resources I am especially familiar with and consider reputable, but each has its own strengths and limitations you will need to weigh carefully.

Figure 1:

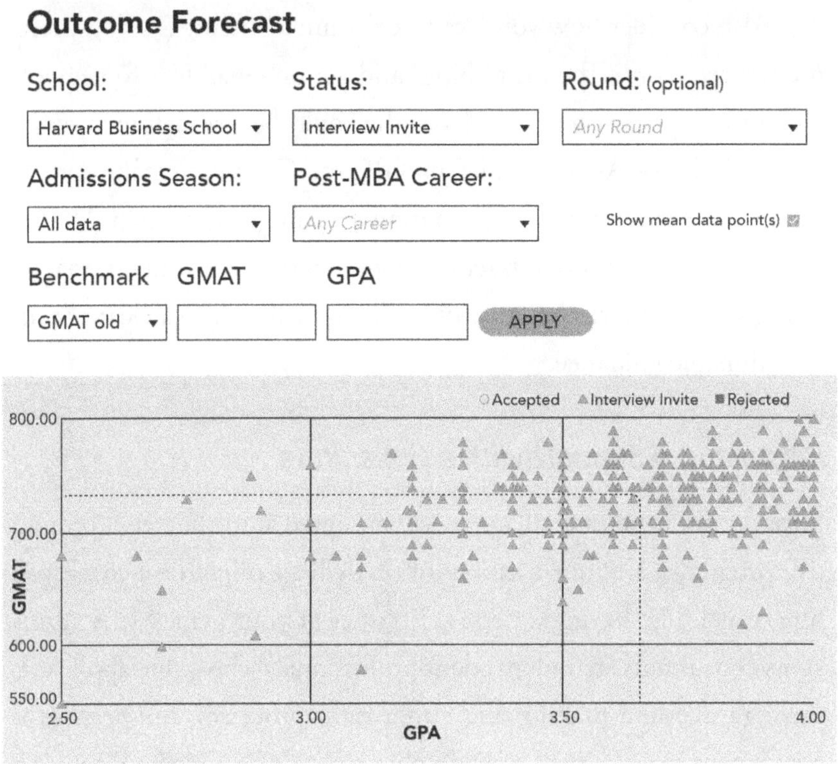

Outcome Forecast

School: [Harvard Business School ▼]   Status: [Interview Invite ▼]   Round: (optional) [*Any Round* ▼]

Admissions Season: [All data ▼]   Post-MBA Career: [*Any Career* ▼]   Show mean data point(s) ☑

Benchmark [GMAT old ▼]   GMAT [   ]   GPA [   ]   (APPLY)

Here's a snapshot of the Clear Admit's MBA LiveWire interactive feed, where you can check the status of business school admissions in real time. Source: Clearadmit.com, retrieved June 3, 2025.

Navigating the Online Resource Maze

While abundant resources help applicants, they can also create information overload. If you've searched online or asked around for advice about applying to business school, you might feel overwhelmed by conflicting opinions. With such an abundance of options, your challenge isn't finding information; it's curating it.

As you explore each source, focus on consistency (Are multiple sources pointing to the same core advice?), credibility (Does the author have verifiable admissions experience?), and practicality (Can you immediately apply the tip to your own profile?).

Also consider how you like to consume content. Do you prefer the written word? Then read blogs and get on email lists for schools. Prefer to watch or listen? Check out the YouTube channels mentioned above. A fan of AI? Consult ChatGPT or Grok, but make sure to watch out for erroneous information you might get when AI "hallucinates." The point is to filter the resources through your criteria. By doing so, you'll turn the noise of too many voices into a clear chorus of actionable guidance.

Personalized Support with a Consultant

I always say it takes a village to get accepted into the very competitive programs, and one member of that village might be a coach you hire, much like having a personal trainer at your gym. MBA admissions consultants are independent professionals who guide applicants through decision-making and application processes. *Independent* is a key word here, as they provide objective advice and should not be affiliated with any business school, other than possibly being an alum.

Consultants help you consider your academic background, work experience, and career goals so you can decide which schools to target and can craft the best application strategy, including choosing round timing, balancing reach and safety schools, and deciding whether to reapply if needed. They also offer guidance on your résumé and essays, help you prepare for interviews, and partner with you on decisions of which offer to accept.

With respect to services, you'll see that consultants offer hourly rates, à la carte options, comprehensive packages, or a combination of these. Single essay review or interview prep are examples of à la carte offerings, while comprehensive packages might include school selection guidance, essay editing, interview prep, and unlimited revisions. Fees for the various services typically range from a few hundred to several thousand dollars.[7] Some engagements can even reach five-digit figures.

Regardless of the engagement you choose, you'll benefit from having an expert in your corner. The process is daunting, and I have witnessed the anxiety that many applicants have to manage on the admissions journey. I remember one client breaking out in hives before her group interview at Wharton. I've seen applicants withdraw for days after getting rejected when they were certain of getting accepted. To make the process easier to get through, I suggest equipping yourself with an understanding of the other side of this journey. I know that the fear of failure or disappointment from not getting something we want doesn't go away easily. But understanding that the process is not a proxy for your self-worth can give you the strength to keep moving forward.

---

7   "How Much Does Applying for an MBA Cost?," *QS TopMBA*, updated December 9, 2022, https://www.topmba.com/blog/how-much-does-applying-mba-cost.

A More Agile Admissions Process

MBA admissions leaders increasingly find themselves needing to respond to, and sometimes capitalize on, the rapidly changing landscape around them. Understanding the role this agility plays in the life of a business school can be empowering for applicants.

In earlier eras, admissions calendars, testing requirements, and program offerings seemed almost immutable: three admissions rounds per year, a hard GMAT score cutoff, and a fixed two-year, full-time program structure. Now, admissions practices are much less rigid, with schools sometimes adjusting in real time, revising deadlines, waiving or reintroducing standardized tests, launching new program formats, and rebranding their messaging in response to economic, social, and technological developments.

Many of these changes work in applicants' favor with the greater flexibility they may bring, but keeping track of it all can be confusing and frustrating. Let's look at just what the schools are responding to and how they are responding so you can feel more in control and informed.

THE AGILITY IMPERATIVE FOR BUSINESS SCHOOLS

External forces continuously shape business school policies. These forces compel them to adapt their admissions strategies in response.

Public Policy and Politics

Changes in government policies and political climates can have immediate effects on applicant pools. For example, visa restrictions or shifts in international relations may deter prospective students from certain regions, prompting schools to adjust outreach efforts or waive specific requirements to maintain enrollment diversity. When administrations implement new regulations, whether related to immigration, higher-education funding, or workplace rules, programs must pivot quickly, sometimes revising admissions criteria or deadlines mid-cycle to account for newly eligible or ineligible candidates.

In recent years, MBA admissions have increasingly become entangled in high-stakes policy battles, forcing business schools to adapt on the fly. Case in point: In May 2025, the Trump administration targeted Harvard with a sweeping campaign, freezing $2.3 billion in federal research funding, threatening to revoke its tax-exempt status, and notifying the US Department of Homeland Security that Harvard's Student and Exchange Visitor Program (SEVP) certification was revoked. That meant Harvard would lose its legal authority to issue I-20 forms, which academic institutions must provide in order for F-1 and J-1 visa holders to secure and maintain their student status. Without SEVP certification, current international students could no longer demonstrate lawful enrollment, and incoming students could not obtain visas to study at Harvard, effectively barring Harvard's 6,800 international enrollees from US campuses.[8]

In June, courts issued temporary restraining orders blocking the policy, allowing Harvard to resume enrolling international students, and Harvard announced that new admitted international students could defer their enrollment.[9] Then, in September, a presidential proclamation imposed a $100,000 fee on new H-1B petitions. This added cost to employers is likely to deter sponsorship for international MBAs and shrink full-time US offers.

---

8   Maya Yang, "Trump Administration Halts Harvard's Ability to Enroll International Students," *The Guardian*, May 22, 2025, https://www.theguardian.com/us-news/2025/may/22/trump-harvard-international-students.

9   Collin Binkley and Fu Ting, "Judge Puts Temporary Hold on Trump's Latest Ban on Harvard's Foreign Students," *AP News*, June 7, 2025, https://apnews.com/article/bb3cf204111567927cf37b63e5927582.

The back-and-forth of this saga, which one admissions expert described as "unprecedented uncertainty,"[10] shows how political directives around immigration enforcement not only impact applicants and current students but significantly disrupt the day-to-day running of a business school.

A year earlier, in response to the Supreme Court's ban on race-conscious admissions, Yale SOM overhauled its procedures. It eliminated race as a factor in financial aid, barred access to applicants' check-box racial data, and retrained admissions officers to ensure full compliance, illustrating the ripple effects of affirmative action litigation on elite MBA pipelines.[11]

The following additional examples underscore the point that business schools aren't living in a bubble and that continual upheaval requires constant monitoring and agility of admissions policies.

Public Health Events

The COVID-19 pandemic vividly illustrated how health crises force schools to be nimble. As testing centers closed and travel restrictions took hold, schools recognized that rigid deadlines and GMAT-only policies risked excluding strong candidates. By shifting to test-optional formats and creating flexible admissions windows, programs ensured continuity in recruiting despite volatile circumstances.

---

10   Marlena Corcoran, "Top Admissions Experts Weigh In on Harvard International Student Ban," *Forbes*, May 27, 2025, https://www.forbes.com/sites/marlenacorcoran/2025/05/27/top-admissions-experts-on-international-student-ban-at-harvard/.

11   James Paterson, "MBA Programs Recruiting Students from Untraditional Backgrounds," *Higher Ed Dive*, July 10, 2018, https://www.highereddive.com/news/mba-programs-recruiting-students-from-untraditional-backgrounds/527372/.

Globalization and Mobility

Today's applicants are more globally mobile than ever, relocating across regions for work or lifestyle reasons. In response, business schools have diversified program formats—launching online MBAs, part-time and modular offerings, and deferred-enrollment tracks—to meet candidates wherever they are. This shift acknowledges that mobility isn't just about physical relocation; it reflects new expectations around work-life balance and learning on one's own terms.

Industry Trends

Layoffs, economic downturns, and technological disruptions also drive admissions agility. During tech-sector layoffs in 2022 and 2023, several schools announced GMAT waivers targeting displaced professionals, which some considered a savvy move that both supported affected candidates and expanded the applicant pool. Similarly, as industries such as healthcare, finance, and energy have evolved, schools have introduced specialized tracks and certificate programs to align with emerging market needs. For applicants, this means staying informed about evolving deadlines, criteria, and program options, because what appears settled today may change tomorrow in service of a school's strategic priorities.

Business schools have demonstrated their agility in the face of these external forces with changes in standardized testing policies, offering more MBA program formats to respond to an increasingly mobile candidate pool, changing who they view as an ideal candidate, and addressing the rise of AI in the application process and their own recruiting practices. The remainder of this section takes a deeper dive into those examples of agility so you can consider how to use these shifts to your advantage.

EVOLVING TEST POLICIES AND TARGETS

For decades, the GMAT was the universal gatekeeper. If you wanted an MBA, you took the GMAT. But as application volume grew more global and diverse, schools began accepting the GRE. GMAC launched the Executive Assessment to give seasoned professionals a more tailored, time-efficient readiness check for executive MBA (EMBA) and specialized master's tracks before extending it to full-time MBA programs at business schools as well. New York University's Stern School of Business (NYU Stern) began accepting this assessment in 2019.[12]

Then, schools began rolling out test-optional and waiver policies for experienced hires, exceptional undergraduates, and candidates from certain backgrounds, driven not only by accessibility concerns but by a desire to attract diverse cohorts. They have also offered test waivers for candidates affected by unusual circumstances, such as tech-sector layoffs, or for those who already had a comparable proof point such as MCAT or LSAT scores. This pattern was also seen during the COVID-19 pandemic, when schools added a third application round, extended deadlines, and loosened testing requirements almost overnight.

In each of these cases, admissions offices adjusted out of necessity to secure a pipeline of qualified candidates in a shifting environment.

RISING SCORES, RISING STRESS

While testing flexibility is a welcome change for many applicants, the flip side is that competition has intensified. Application volume

---

12 NYU Stern, "NYU Stern School of Business Now Accepting GMAC's Executive Assessment as Part of Full-Time MBA Application," press release, August 19, 2019, https://www.stern.nyu.edu/experience-stern/news-events/nyu-stern-school-business-now-accepting-gmac-s-executive-assessment-part-full-time-mba-application.

tends to increase when barriers such as test scores are removed. Also, as schools keep a close eye on their rankings, which get a boost when they admit applicants with the highest test scores, average GMAT and GRE benchmarks have steadily climbed. This makes each point gain more consequential, putting added pressure on applicants to chase ever-higher percentiles and possibly discouraging many from applying in the first place.

The result of all this movement—choices of tests to take, optional score submission, and rising score expectations—is a more nuanced testing landscape in which understanding each school's specific use of scores is as important as the test choice and the scores themselves. You'll learn more about this as relevant to your own situation in chapter 5: Your Application Strategy.

MOBILITY FUELS AGILITY IN MBA ADMISSIONS

The world is a more mobile place now: Technology enabled remote work, and the COVID-19 pandemic normalized it. A physician in Boston can go for an EMBA in Paris.[13] A father of young sons can commute from Pocatello, Idaho, to his EMBA at Yale.[14] A marketing manager in Mumbai can complete an online degree at a top US school while staying home in India.

Admissions offices have responded by courting globally mobile candidates through virtual information sessions, region-focused webinars, and international alumni panels as they aim to meet candidates where they are, digitally and geographically. This expansion of applicant

---

13   "Successfully Balancing Work, Life, and Study in the HEC Paris EMBA Program," HEC Paris, May 23, 2023, https://www.hec.edu/en/executive-mba/news/successfully-balancing-work-life-and-study-in-the-hec-paris-emba-program.

14   "A Day in the Life: Blake Christensen '26," Yale School of Management, April 14, 2025, https://som.yale.edu/story/2025/day-life-blake-christensen-26?utm_campaign=apr2025&utm_medium=email&utm_source=newsletter.

pools means a more dynamic, interesting environment with classmates bringing life experiences and worldviews from, well, literally all over the world. But it also means increased competition for applicants.

MORE PROGRAM FORMAT CHOICES

Traditional full-time, two-year MBAs completed on campus are still the anchor of most business schools, but part-time, evening, online, executive, and deferred-enrollment pathways have proliferated to meet diverse candidate needs. In 2019, Harvard's 2+2 program targeted STEM undergraduates, locking in offers before they even graduated and entered the workforce, giving them two to five years to enroll if accepted. Other schools expanded their online and hybrid MBA options to appeal to professionals who don't want to uproot themselves. Suddenly, someone who moved to a farm in rural Vermont during the COVID-19 pandemic and doesn't want to leave, or an American expat based in London, can stay put.

For example, the Walter A. Haas School of Business at the University of California, Berkeley (Berkeley Haas) has a "Flex" offering with online or hybrid options for the evening and weekend MBA so you don't have to relocate to the Bay Area. In August 2022, the first blended learning option was offered by Wharton's MBA Program for Executives to increase accessibility for rising leaders anywhere in the world. By offering more flexible formats, schools both broaden their reach and buffer against fluctuations in candidate demographics.

The power dynamic has shifted from *Which of a small number of schools will accept me?* to *Where do I choose to go?*

Back when I was choosing a part-time MBA program in Boston, the top choices that came to mind were Boston University and Boston College because they were within commuting distance. Today, I would also be able to consider other business schools across the country, such as Berkeley Haas on the opposite coast. The power dynamic has shifted from *Which of a small number of schools will accept me?* to *Where do I choose to go?*

A Guide to MBA Program Formats

Full-Time MBA

A two-year, campus-based program designed for early- to mid-career professionals who pause full-time work to immerse themselves in coursework, case studies, networking, and internships. This format emphasizes cohort learning, on-campus activities, and summer internships to accelerate career pivots and leadership development.

Part-Time and Evening MBA

Structured for working professionals who wish to earn their degree while maintaining a full-time job. Classes are typically held evenings and/or weekends over three to five years, so they are less disruptive to a career. These programs still offer access to career services and campus events.

Online MBA

A fully remote or hybrid format that delivers the core MBA curriculum via virtual classes, asynchronous lessons, and periodic on-campus residencies. Ideal for self-motivated learners seeking flexibility, an online program allows students to balance work, family, and study from anywhere in the world.

Executive MBA (EMBA)

A modular program tailored to senior managers and executives with significant professional experience (often over ten years). EMBAs comprise intensive weekend or block-format sessions, focusing on strategic leadership, advanced management skills, and peer learning among seasoned professionals.

Deferred Enrollment (e.g., HBS 2+2 and Chicago Booth Scholars Program)

A pathway for current undergraduates or early-career entrants to secure an MBA seat in advance. After admission, candidates complete two to four years of work experience before matriculating. This option helps future applicants lock in a top-tier spot while building their professional profile.

BEING SMART ABOUT AI

Incorporating AI is a work in progress in terms of how programs recruit and evaluate applicants, so it's no surprise that schools are grappling with how far they want to go. Some programs are cautiously piloting AI in their admissions offices, but nearly everyone agrees on one core value: The process must not lose its humanity. Some worry that if AI is given too much control, it might miss the nuance and context of candidates from unconventional or underrepresented backgrounds.

Beyond internal use, schools are also navigating how applicants themselves are engaging with AI tools such as ChatGPT. There is not a unified stance. Some programs openly acknowledge that this is the way the world is and encourage applicants to use AI tools, particularly to brainstorm or create outlines for their essays, as long as the ideas and voice remain their own. Others take a firmer line, explicitly discouraging any AI involvement in application materials.

MBA programs are on the cusp of transformation, aware of the efficiencies AI can bring but wary of eroding the authenticity that is critical to the admissions process. For now, the consensus is to proceed with caution, enhancing, not replacing, human judgment with the help of technology.

Strategic Moves in Admissions

Business schools rarely alter their admissions criteria and practices without a clear purpose. Why fix what isn't broken? Yet in recent years, programs have deliberately redefined the ideal candidate, shifting away from purely quantitative metrics toward a more holistic assessment of qualities that align with each school's long-term vision and values. They also have heightened awareness of their own bottom line. After all, a business school needs to be sustainable, too.

SEEKING MORE THAN SMARTS

Not long ago, an MBA application was judged almost exclusively on numbers: stellar GMAT scores, perfect GPAs, and a linear career trajectory. High scores bolster a program's brand because schools can use rising averages to signal their prestige, but this discourages talented applicants whose strengths lie outside standardized tests. By offering GMAT waivers or accepting alternative assessments as discussed earlier regarding agility, schools intentionally broaden their applicant pools to include demographics that historically underperform on standardized exams.

Admissions committees want to know the following:

- What life experiences does this applicant bring, and what have they learned from them?

- How will they enhance their peers' learning by bringing those life experiences?

- Will they enrich the school's culture and advance its mission?

Rather than simply chasing ever-higher scores, programs now prioritize diverse life experiences, leadership potential, and cultural contributions.

SOCIAL IMPACT

Business schools have elevated social impact from a peripheral theme to a core mission, believing that business plays a key role in addressing societal challenges. In February 2023, more than seven hundred business school deans gathered at a conference to explore the question, "How can we redefine leadership for positive societal impact?" and to align curricula with purpose-driven competencies rather than purely financial outcomes.[15]

HBS's mission, "We educate leaders who make a difference in the world," and Stanford GSB's "Change Lives. Change Organizations. Change the World" exemplify this shift, as does Yale SOM's "Educating Leaders for Business and Society" and INSEAD's emphasis on "responsible leaders who transform business and society."

Applicants today may have a competitive advantage if they can show credible social impact track records or clear commitments to

---

15 "Forging the Future of Business Education," Association to Advance Collegiate Schools of Business, February 17, 2023, https://www.aacsb.edu/insights/articles/2023/02/forging-the-future-of-business-education.

positive change. Admissions committees now look for evidence of community engagement, nonprofit or public sector experience, and entrepreneurial projects aimed at societal benefit. Consequently, successful candidates include those who craft essays and interviews around personal values and societal challenges, showing a commitment to help advance both the school's mission and the broader public good.

NAVIGATING GLOBALLY

Shifting geopolitical landscapes—trade agreements, Brexit, new economic blocs—have reshaped how business schools think about the value of a truly international cohort. The MBA classroom today is a microcosm of a global marketplace, as students learn how others see the world, a crucial aspect of leadership on a global stage. Business schools proudly showcase the number of countries represented, with international students often making up 30 to 50 percent of incoming classes. When business schools boast about how many nations are represented in their cohorts, they signal a commitment to fostering global understanding. But this isn't just window dressing; it's strategic. Schools know that graduates will navigate cross-border teams, supply chains, and markets, and the more effectively they do that, and the more of a visible impact they make, the more the school's reputation will be enhanced.

If you come from a country that is less represented in the student body, you could have a slight edge in the admissions process, assuming your application is competitive in other respects. An applicant from a relatively underrepresented country—say, Belize—might gain a marginal advantage, not because of preferential treatment but because for many schools, building cohorts of students who might otherwise not have a chance to cross paths and share vastly different worldviews is a priority for developing empathic leaders.

At the same time, the top tier is getting more crowded, as schools such as Yale SOM and Duke Fuqua have climbed in rankings position, thanks to some consequential deans at the helm. And US-based students have broadened their sights beyond domestic programs. Europe and Asia have therefore invested heavily to attract American applicants. The resulting competition has prompted top US schools to intensify global recruitment efforts in recent decades, hosting virtual events in emerging markets, translating marketing materials into multiple languages, and building alumni networks worldwide. This global context means more competition, more diversity in applicant backgrounds, and more need for you to differentiate yourself.

The globalization of cohorts brings its own challenges as visa policies, political mandates, and economic downturns add layers of complexity to recruiting and building an MBA class.

A NEW PROFESSIONAL PEDIGREE

Elite consulting firms and major financial institutions have long been feeder industries for prestigious business schools, but over the past decade, schools have deliberately sought to broaden their intake to mirror shifting industry demands. For example, technology now consistently joins consulting and financial services as one of the three top hiring sectors for MBA graduates, with tech's share rising sharply as firms such as Amazon and Google invest in general management talent, not just engineers.[16]

Admissions committees are also increasingly seeking applicants with nontraditional backgrounds. For example, museum curators, sports figures, and those who've participated in Teach for America,

---

16 Marc Ethier, "Strong MBA Hiring Forecast in New GMAC Survey of Recruiters," *Poets & Quants*, July 1, 2024, https://poetsandquants.com/2024/07/01/strong-mba-hiring-forecast-in-new-gmac-survey-of-recruiters/.

to name just a few, bring a welcoming diversity of worldviews and skill sets. With leadership development a primary focus of business schools, programs recognize that all areas of the economy, from the corporate sector to nonprofits, benefit when a variety of perspectives informs their leadership.

FINANCIAL CONSIDERATIONS IN ADMISSIONS

At the end of the day, business schools operate like businesses even though they are institutions of higher education. With their goal of developing leaders who will go out and change the world, they must attract the best and brightest candidates with the potential to be changemakers, and they have to recruit and retain faculty who can teach and mentor those changemakers. So, behind every tweak to the admissions strategy lies an intentional business decision, with institutional changes typically being responses to specific competitive or financial pressures.

Today's deans, for example, are as much fundraisers as they are guardians of academic reputation. One of their top jobs is to build relationships with alumni, secure large gifts, and drive scholarship endowments. They cultivate donors by showcasing shiny new buildings and innovative research centers (which cost money), and when a high-profile gift goes viral in the media, that signals to prospective applicants and supporters alike that a school is on an upward trajectory.

Your Bottom Line

The strategic considerations covered in this chapter from the admissions perspective underscore a simple truth: Admissions is never just about who you, the applicant, are. It's also about how you will advance the institution's mission and impact the bottom line.

Schools operate in a competitive marketplace, balancing their mission-driven values with financial imperatives. As an applicant, you're part of that equation. When you understand these strategic forces, you can position yourself not only as a qualified candidate but as someone who aligns with the institution's goals.

So, what does all this mean for you?

LEVERAGE INFORMATION WISELY

Gone are the days of blind submissions. With real-time data on acceptances, waiting lists, and yield trends in chat rooms and industry websites, you can track where you stand and avoid unnecessary guesswork. Use that transparency to refine your timing, target schools, and manage your expectations.

ADAPT TO SHIFTING CRITERIA

Admissions criteria can, and do, change mid-cycle in response to global events, industry shifts, and competitive pressures. Stay vigilant for testing-policy updates, new program launches, or sudden waivers, and be prepared to pivot your strategy if an unexpected opportunity arises.

ALIGN WITH INSTITUTIONAL STRATEGY

Each school fine-tunes its criteria to attract candidates who serve its mission—whether that's global leadership, social impact, or cutting-edge innovation. Your task is to demonstrate how your background, voice, and ambitions fit into that narrative, not just to rack up impressive metrics on paper.

THINK GLOBALLY, ACT LOCALLY

As cohorts become more international, your lived experience can be a differentiator, especially if you hail from an underrepresented region or industry. At the same time, recognize that you face more competition than ever before. Cultivate a distinct personal brand that highlights not only your achievements but also your unique life experience.

CHOOSE FROM AN EXPANDED MENU OF FORMATS

With full-time, part-time, online, executive, and deferred-enrollment options, you have unprecedented flexibility. But with choice comes complexity. You must weigh trade-offs between lifestyle, career trajectory, and program culture. Identify the format that aligns best with your professional and personal goals and remember that flexibility often yields a stronger sense of control.

POSITION YOURSELF STRATEGICALLY

Schools balance their mission-driven objectives with financial objectives—scholarship arms races, alumni fundraising, and brand positioning all factor into admission decisions. Understand that your candidacy is part of a broader equation. By demonstrating both academic readiness and cultural fit, you increase your odds of receiving not just an offer, but also meaningful financial support should you need it.

YOUR STRATEGIC SWOT

As mentioned in the introduction of this book, each chapter will close with this twist on the popular strategic analysis framework for evaluating strengths, weaknesses, opportunities, and threats (SWOT). I encourage you to conduct your own SWOT to apply what you learn in each chapter as relevant for your unique circumstances. Here are your chapter 1 SWOT questions:

Have you been operating under outdated assumptions about how MBA admissions work, or have you been getting outdated advice? Which aspects of the current reality might signal the need to change your strategy?

How can you respond to the changing balance of power between applicants and schools? Does the power dynamic alter your strategy or the emotional side of considering or applying for an MBA?

Considering the range of types of programs and deferred-enrollment options, do you have more choices than you were aware of? Which ones might be worth considering more seriously?

CHAPTER 2

The Stakeholder Web

A re MBA candidates products or customers? When applying to business school, they might feel like customers armed with the power of the purse. They shop for programs at recruitment fairs, evaluate options based on media rankings, and try to make the best investment for their futures, informed by school websites and chatroom threads. But as soon as they hit submit on the application, that feeling starts to shift. They're no longer the ones in control—they're the "products" being chosen. Schools look at how an applicant's contribution will shape classroom learning, how their story enhances the school's brand, and how their post-MBA success will impact rankings and employer relationships.

This is where many applicants get stuck. They assume rejection comes from a single grade in a college transcript, one essay that didn't resonate, or an interviewer who didn't like them. But that's rarely the whole story. Admissions decisions are almost never about any one moment or one person. They're about alignment across a much broader set of priorities, most of which live outside the applicant's view.

This chapter examines how these diverse priorities shape admissions decisions. The admissions office may be the one communicating your final decision, but they're operating within a much larger ecosystem shaped by deans, donors, career services, faculty, alumni, current students, media coverage, and even political and legal pressures. These stakeholders all bring different interests and expectations to the table. Collectively, as what I call the *stakeholder web*, they shape not only who gets admitted but what kind of class and program a school wants to build.

In this web of power dynamics and competing interests, you're not just presenting yourself to one committee; you're presenting yourself to a constellation of needs, ambitions, constraints, and agendas. In other words: It's not all about you!

Profiles in Power

Chapter 1 introduced the idea that business schools don't operate in a vacuum. Macro forces are at work, with employers, the media, and public policy all playing roles in shaping business schools' strategies. Within schools, faculty, deans, students, and alumni can have a say in the strategic direction of programs and who gets in. Now we're going to drill deeper into those dynamics with "Profiles in Power" for insight into the complex web of stakeholder relationships and perspectives.

Fueling the Talent Pipeline

When it comes to MBA admissions, employers and the career services office don't just wait at the finish line. They shape the race. Let's look at their influence.

THE EMPLOYERS BEHIND THE CURTAIN

When you apply to an MBA program, you might think you are only writing for the admissions committee. But you are also writing for another audience. Employers may not sit on admissions committees, but their influence stretches all the way upstream. They shape expectations, tweak desired skill sets, and sometimes even influence who gets a second look.

Three industries dominate MBA hiring: consulting, finance, and tech. Top firms in each sector are prominent recruiters, and their preferences carry serious weight. When a recruiter from Boston Consulting Group (BCG) or Morgan Stanley mentions they want more hires with advanced data analytics or AI fluency, that feedback doesn't just stay in the career office. It makes its way back to admissions, sometimes indirectly, sometimes very directly.

Top Employers by Volume and Influence

Consulting giants such as McKinsey & Company, Bain & Company, and Boston Consulting Group (BCG) remain the most frequent MBA employers, especially at top-tier programs. At Chicago Booth, for example, BCG hired forty-eight full-time MBAs in 2024—more than any other employer. Also at Booth, Amazon was ranked fourth, while finance powerhouses such as Goldman Sachs and JPMorganChase were also in the top ten.[17] Sector-wide trends support this concentration of hiring power. According to a recent survey by GMAC and Career Services & Employer Alliance (CSEA), 93 percent of tech companies, 86 percent of consulting firms, and 75 percent of finance firms reported plans to hire MBAs, with nearly one-third of consulting and tech firms planning to increase their MBA hiring year over year.[18]

BOARDROOM INFLUENCE, BACK-CHANNEL POWER

Employer influence doesn't stop at the recruiting table. Many top firms are represented on the advisory boards of business schools, creating yet another channel through which industry feedback reaches deans and leadership. Georgetown University's McDonough School of Business,

---

17 "Major Employers 2024," Chicago Booth, September 1, 2024, https://www.chicago-booth.edu/employmentreport/employer/2024-employer.

18 *Corporate Recruiters Survey 2024 Report*, Graduate Management Admission Council, 2024, https://www.gmac.com/-/media/files/gmac/research/employment-outlook/2024-corporate-recruiters-survey/2024_gmac_crs_report.pdf?rev=43588bf ef9a549af9bb00a432a3d7b06.

for instance, features MBA alumni advisory board members from Accenture, KPMG, Marriott, Pfizer, and other major employers.[19] These relationships can shape everything from curriculum design to strategic planning, and inevitably, admissions strategy, too.

Sometimes feedback bypasses formal channels entirely. Alumni who work at top firms often act as informal ambassadors and can inform the school when they believe a recent graduate underperformed or a recruiting experience went awry. These conversations rarely make headlines, but they do shape institutional decisions behind the scenes.

CAREER SERVICES: THE HIDDEN POWER BROKER

Career services offices are among the most powerful players in the MBA ecosystem. They serve as the bridge between employer demand and institutional supply, translating real-time market signals into long-term admissions and curriculum strategy. These teams gather intel from recruiters, monitor post-MBA hiring trends, and often participate in shaping the profile of incoming classes. In some schools, they even sit in on admissions committee meetings, which serves as a subtle but potent reminder that every admitted student needs to be market-ready.

Their influence is far from informal. Through professional associations such as CSEA, career services teams aggregate employer feedback, benchmark hiring data, and identify emerging skill gaps. This information doesn't just help students land jobs but can flow directly into curriculum adjustments and admissions priorities. The impact on rankings is just as direct. Career services compile the employment reports that feed into major MBA rankings. A number

---

19   "MBA Alumni Advisory Council," McDonough School of Business, https://msb. georgetown.edu/alumni/mba-alumni-advisory-council/.

of these rankings place heavy emphasis on short-term salary outcomes and job placement percentages. In the *Financial Times* 2025 global MBA ranking, for instance, 16 percent of a full-time MBA program's ranking is based on weighted salary, defined as the average alumni salary three years after completion. Another 16 percent of the ranking is based on salary increase—the average difference in alumni salary from before the MBA to present. Both weighted salary and salary increase are the top two metrics in the ranking.[20]

The bottom line is this: If students are not getting hired, or not getting hired at high enough salaries, schools can slip in the rankings, and that affects how the next class of applicants and other key stakeholders such as alumni donors and corporate recruiters view the program.

CAREER OUTCOMES AS CURRENCY

Ultimately, the relationship between employers, career services, and admissions is symbiotic. Career services relies on admissions to bring in students who can succeed in the job market and boost placement stats. Admissions relies on career services to generate outcomes that validate the school's selectivity and market appeal, especially by helping to boost rankings. And employers rely on both to maintain the quality of their MBA talent pipeline.

I experienced this firsthand when I oversaw admissions at a British business school. The career services director was nervous when I wanted to admit someone who was a strong candidate academically but wasn't as marketable for the job market in an obvious way. The applicant could be thousands of miles away, but the careers manager was two doors down from my office, and I had to work with her every day, which was (truthfully) a factor in my decision-making.

---

20   Leo Cremonezi et al., "FT Global MBA Ranking 2025: Methodology and Key," *Financial Times*, February 16, 2025, https://www.ft.com/mba-method.

Calling the Shots: Faculty as Stakeholders

Are you my boss?

That's what I wanted to say, with a side-eye, when an imposing strategy professor educated at the University of Cambridge marched into my admissions office like a general in the British armed forces and told me to admit an applicant he met at a prospective student event on campus. As someone who had previously worked for a large American corporation with a clear organizational chart, I was surprised. I reported to the administrative director of MBA programs—a former London banker who traded cutthroat corporate life for a pastoral farm in the English countryside. Or did I? This didn't make sense until twenty years later when an assistant dean of admissions at an elite M7 school told me she saw herself as working for the faculty.

I came to appreciate that the admissions office does (indirectly) work for the faculty. After all, the admissions team is recruiting and admitting students (or "products") who will be taught by the faculty. If the students aren't academically strong or lack solid work experience, that creates a problem for the professor teaching the class. Given that the faculty hold all the power in higher education, it's prudent to keep them happy.

You might be wondering, Do faculty *really* hold all the power? Well, in theory, the faculty are collectively just one stakeholder among many, but in practice, they wield immense influence. Some of it is indirect—shaping curriculum, setting the academic bar, pushing for new programs that require new kinds of students. But sometimes, their influence on admissions is not so subtle, like with the strategy professor I mentioned earlier. In my time working in admissions, I also encountered an applicant who had great business connections that could benefit the school but who lacked strong academic credentials. The admissions committee took a leap of faith and admitted the applicant, but it didn't take long for faculty to complain that the student was struggling with the quantitative coursework, and those complaints made their way back to the admissions office.

The Influential Voice of Current Students

Students are often the first people you'll meet on your MBA journey, whether at admit weekends, info sessions, or on a campus tour. Their informal feedback can influence how admissions views you, especially when it comes to fit and interpersonal presence. I've seen admissions ask current students for their opinion on applicants from their home country when the academic or professional experience on the résumé is not familiar. In some business schools, such as the University of California, Los Angeles Anderson School of Management (UCLA Anderson), second-year MBA students participate in the interview process for the full-time MBA program.[21]

So, that casual—or formal—conversation you have with a current student about why you want an MBA? Don't underestimate it!

---

21   Emily Tu, "First Year Perspectives: Getting Ready for Your MBA Admissions Interview," UCLA Anderson School of Management, January 22, 2025, https://stories.anderson.ucla.edu/mba-insider/first-year-perspectives-getting-ready-for-your-mba-admissions-interview/.

Alumni: Guardians of Legacy and Stewards of Brand

When I worked in admissions in the UK, I flew from London to Munich to attend an MBA fair organized by GMAC. As I was unpacking in my hotel room, I turned on CNN International and happened to hear a taped interview with the dean of London Business School (LBS) talking about the powerful influence of their alumni network. He commented on how alumni "wear the LBS brand" proudly on their sleeve.

That moment stuck with me because it reflects a truth I've observed across all prestigious MBA programs: Alumni carry deep pride in their school and often hold significant influence behind the scenes. Alumni care deeply about rankings, in part because those numbers reflect on their own résumés and professional reputations. Furthermore, many are financial stakeholders, serving on advisory boards or making major donations that can change the trajectory of a school. Some go a step further by writing recommendation letters for applicants or directly advocating their candidacy with admissions officers or deans.

Their influence blends personal pride, sentimentality, and strategy. When rankings slip or programs shift direction, alumni aren't shy about voicing concerns. For many, an MBA is not just a degree; it's part of their identity. So, while alumni don't usually sit on admissions committees, their voices are far from absent. They shape reputation, reinforce tradition, and may apply pressure behind the scenes.

Donors Who Shape Programs

"This is a once-in-a-lifetime chance to give back to the School and help it continue to push the boundaries of excellence in management education."[22]

That is how Nike co-founder and Stanford GSB alumnus Phil Knight described his $400 million donation to Stanford University in 2016—one of the largest individual gifts ever to a university at that time. His gift established the Knight-Hennessy Scholars program, a graduate-level scholarship program to develop a new generation of global leaders by bringing top students from around the world to Stanford for fully funded graduate education, including at the business school. (This was just ten years after he'd donated $105 million to the business school to fund state-of-the-art buildings!)

Knight described his vision as a community of future leaders committed to the greater good. Though the Knight-Hennessy Scholars program serves all of Stanford's graduate schools, its emphasis on interdisciplinary collaboration and civic-minded leadership subtly reinforces similar priorities at the GSB. While Stanford GSB has long prized innovation and entrepreneurial thinking, this gift helped legitimize and support applicants with more mission-driven goals. It may not have shifted the majority of graduates into public service, but it created space for more values-driven candidates to gain admission and thrive.

Whether through Phil Knight's transformative gifts at Stanford or other major donations, such as Stephen M. Ross's $200 million to the

---

22   "Nike Founder Phil Knight to Give $105 Million to Stanford GSB," Stanford Graduate School of Business, August 1, 2006, https://www.gsb.stanford.edu/newsroom/school-news/nike-founder-phil-knight-give-105-million-stanford-gsb.

University of Michigan's Ross School of Business[23] or Marion Anderson's $100 million to the business school at UCLA,[24] philanthropy often leaves a lasting imprint on MBA programs. While these contributions are publicly framed as altruistic investments in education, they often come with an implicit influence on institutional priorities or even program name changes. For example, in the spring of 2025, the EMBA program at Chicago Booth School of Business received a $100 million donation from alumnus Konstantin Sokolov, MBA '05, the largest ever made to Booth. The program was renamed to the Sokolov Executive MBA Program in his honor.[25]

In elite MBA programs, that influence may extend to what gets funded, which values are elevated, and even who gets admitted. Strings may not be pulled, but there is a possibility that they could be attached.

23   "U-Michigan to Receive $200 Million from Prominent Real Estate Developer," *University of Michigan News*, September 4, 2013, https://news.umich.edu/u-michigan-to-receive-200-million-from-prominent-real-estate-developer-stephen-m-ross/.

24   Larry Gordon, "UCLA's Anderson School to Get $100-Million Gift from Namesake's Widow," *Los Angeles Times*, May 13, 2015, https://www.latimes.com/local/education/la-me-ucla-gift-20150514-story.html.

25   Celeste Alcalay, "Booth School of Business Receives $100 Million Donation to Executive MBA Program," *The Chicago Maroon*, April 16, 2025, https://chicagomaroon.com/47026/news/booth-school-of-business-receives-100-million-donation-to-executive-mba-program/.

The Media as a Stakeholder

"I'm the first to admit I created a monster, and the monster is uncontrollable. The monster roams the earth doing all kinds of damage to many schools."[26]

This was said by John Byrne, former *BusinessWeek* editor and founder of the influential online graduate management education news site *Poets & Quants*. Byrne is widely credited for being the original godfather of media rankings for MBA programs. In 1988, when he was an editor at *BusinessWeek*, he saw a desire and need among applicants to go beyond the basic data they could easily access, such as acceptance rates and average GPAs and GMAT scores. So, he mailed out paper surveys, literally licking the envelopes himself, to thousands of students, graduates, employers, and business schools to try to get a handle on the real quality of MBA degrees from various programs. As responses came back, he crunched the data manually. From this unglamorous start emerged what would become the first major MBA ranking—a media phenomenon that other publications quickly copied.

Byrne wasn't being hyperbolic with his uncontrollable monster statement. Rankings have given the media outsized power as a stakeholder shaping business school behavior. Rankings are like a performance review that's broadcast to the world. And they don't just shape how applicants choose programs. They influence donor support, trustee confidence, alumni pride, and even a school's ability to attract faculty or justify tuition increases. And when those rankings drop, the world takes note.

---

26   John Byrne, "John Byrne: The Pros and Cons of Business School Rankings,"
      interview by Dan LeClair, Association to Advance Collegiate Schools of
      Business, May 7, 2015, https://www.aacsb.edu/insights/videos/2015/05/
      john-byrne-pros-and-cons-of-business-school-rankings.

The ripple effect can be enormous. A single hit in the rankings can overshadow an entire year of accomplishments. Suddenly, a school that accepted more applicants with lower GMAT scores is fielding calls about whether it's slipping because of a ranking's methodology that considers incoming student test scores. All this had led Byrne to observe that "MBA applicants tend to put far too much importance on rankings in deciding where to get their degrees, and schools take the whole exercise far too seriously, given the limitations and flaws of this or any other ranking."[27]

 PRO TIP: RANK THE RANKINGS

At *Poets & Quants*, Byrne and his team have tried to get to the heart of MBA program quality and outcomes by publishing a composition of select rankings. The *Poets & Quants* list combines the most influential business school rankings in the world: *U.S. News & World Report*, the *Financial Times*, *Bloomberg Businessweek*, LinkedIn, and the Princeton Review. The latter two rankings were added last year after *The Economist* and *Forbes* decided to abandon their MBA ranking projects.

Applicants can do their part, too. Yes, rankings are useful. Do check them as you select which schools to apply to or to decide about offers but dig deeper. Understand the metrics behind the rankings and look at how schools have moved up or down in rank over a period of time rather than just year-to-year fluctuations. Don't get swept up in the headlines.

27   John A. Byrne, "A Nate Silver-Take on the Most Influential MBA Ranking," LinkedIn, November 18, 2012, https://www.linkedin.com/pulse/20121118221106-17970806-a-nate-silver-take-on-the-most-influential-mba-ranking/.

Deans Caught Between a Rock and a Ranking

Deans operate under intense scrutiny from multiple stakeholders, including university presidents, trustees, donors, and even prospective employers, all of whom expect continual growth in rankings, reputation, and revenue.

Their performance is often evaluated by metrics such as applicant volume, yield rates, postgraduation salaries, and media visibility. Rankings, in particular, carry disproportionate weight in annual reviews and fundraising conversations. A jump in rank can lead to increased donations, higher tuition justification, and personal prestige.

Beyond worrying about rankings, deans set strategic priorities and set institutional priorities that influence admissions policies. Deans also manage relationships with donors, corporate partners, and university leadership, and their decisions reflect those relationships. Deans are the face of the school, but they also drive the internal agenda.

When Government Becomes a Stakeholder

There's an old political adage that elections have consequences. Well, that's true not just for the electorate but for elite business schools, too.

As one example, the US Department of Education launched investigations in 2025 into more than fifty colleges and universities, including several top business schools, over concerns that their diversity-related programs may have violated civil rights law. These inquiries may have been administrative in nature, but their impact was anything but. Under threat of losing Title IV funding, some business schools began quietly rebranding or reducing the visibility of DEI offices. Others paused scholarships earmarked for underrepresented students or reconsidered programs designed to support specific identity groups. In notable moves, schools including the University of Chicago Booth School of Business, the McCombs School of Business at the University of Texas at Austin, the Kellogg School of Management at Northwestern University, and the University of Virginia (UVA) Darden School of Business left a long-standing consortium of schools committed to advancing diversity in business education.

Even schools that remain deeply committed to inclusion have found themselves suddenly constrained in how openly they can talk about it. Essay prompts were some of the first things to change. For example, Darden at UVA previously invited candidates in one of their essay questions to describe their experiences with inclusive organizations and communities. But that language was revised, replaced by more neutral prompts such as how candidates "would contribute to the Darden community."

And Duke Fuqua indirectly but clearly addressed the political climate's impact with this statement in their admissions blog in July of 2025.

> As the application for the next class of Duke MBAs opens, I want to start with a simple message: You are welcome here. We're proud of the diverse and global community that defines Team Fuqua. A lot is changing in the world, but one thing that will never change is our interest in getting to know applicants for who they truly are, their unique achievements, and their dreams for the future.[28]

---

28 Allison Jamison, "Emphasizing Authenticity in Our MBA Application," *Duke Daytime MBA Student Blog*, July 10, 2025, https://blogs.fuqua.duke.edu/duke-mba/2025/07/10/allison-jamison/emphasizing-authenticity-in-our-mba-application.

Navigating these political roads is challenging for business schools that know many international students seek out opportunities to broaden their global perspective by earning an MBA in the United States. For example, this student from South Korea at Michigan Ross expressed clear intentions when commenting on what inspired her to pursue a Ross MBA: "I realized that to take the next step in my career, I needed exposure to the US tech ecosystem, where many cutting-edge business models and technologies are being developed. An MBA at this stage will help me build the skills and network to transition into US product management roles and allow me to explore long-term opportunities in entrepreneurship."[29]

Unlike alumni or donors who shape admissions priorities through money and influence, government stakeholders exert pressure through law and enforcement. Regulatory scrutiny can freeze funding, redirect institutional messaging, or force schools to shelve long-standing commitments. For many schools seeking to increase applications from underrepresented populations, these constraints can be challenging. They may want to communicate values-driven ideals but can no longer say so explicitly or structure application questions in ways that would have been standard just a year earlier.

The result? Admissions teams, communications offices, and academic leadership are in a reactive mode, weighing legal exposure against mission alignment.

---

29 "Ambition in Action: Meet the Michigan Ross Full-Time MBA Class of 2027," Michigan Ross, October 20, 2025, https://michiganross.umich.edu/news/ambition-action-meet-michigan-ross-full-time-mba-class-2027.

The Quiet Influence of Admissions Consultants

MBA admissions consultants influence their clients' short list decisions the way Yelp reviews shape diners' restaurant choices. They wield quiet influence by shaping applicants' perceptions, decisions, and most importantly, short lists.

Consultants also spot trends faster than schools often can because they work across geographies, industries, and applicant profiles. Admissions consultants hear what candidates are worried, excited, or skeptical about as they consider applying to or enrolling in various schools—confidences applicants might be hesitant to say to admissions offices directly. So, while schools are focused on the micro— who's applying to *their* programs—consultants see the macro—how applicants feel about a range of programs and what matters to them.

Business schools recognize consultants' influence on applicant decision-making and often engage with the consultant community through information sessions and industry conferences. Schools aren't just choosing students; students are choosing schools. And consultants are sharing their knowledge of the entire MBA admissions space so students can find the best fit. That makes consultants, in their own way, powerful stakeholders in the admissions ecosystem.

Where Is the Admissions Office in All This?

At this point, you may be wondering, Wait—what about the admissions offices? Aren't they the ones making the decisions? Shouldn't they be front and center in this entire chapter? That's a great question. And yes, technically, they're the ones who sign off on "admit" or "deny" (or "wait-list," in some instances). But as you've seen by now, they are far from the only players on the field.

Admissions officers find themselves navigating many of the same stakeholder pressures we've just explored. They field input from faculty, career services, alumni, donors, and even the legal department. They stay attuned to employer feedback and rankings fallout. They're in the crosshairs of competing interests: long-established diversity goals versus new government policies, social impact career goals versus post-MBA salary metrics, and more. They're expected to deliver a class that satisfies everyone, without losing their sanity.

While applicants tend to see admissions offices as gatekeepers, they can also be considered air traffic controllers, scanning for signals, coordinating multiple inputs, and ensuring a smooth landing for all passengers traveling on an anxiety-ridden admissions journey. The work of the admissions office doesn't exist outside the stakeholder web; it sits squarely in the middle of it.

Your Bottom Line

I hope you see now how much schools serve multiple constituencies—some visible, some behind the curtain. What may seem like a random decision by an admissions committee might be a calculated choice that reflects a negotiation between internal politics, external expectations, and institutional goals. And each stakeholder in the web of people and entities who have a say in whether you get in or not has their own interests.

For career services staff, that might mean making sure that a drop in postgrad employment stats doesn't negatively impact their own careers. For the media, it's not just about publishing interesting and informative stories but also about subscriptions and ad space. For the government, it's about advancing a political agenda that fulfills campaign promises. You are not just applying to a school and a program; you are trying to enter a tangled web of competing interests.

Understanding this stakeholder web won't give you total control over the process, but it will help you craft sharper applications and stop blaming yourself for outcomes you can't control. (There's that "it's not all about you" idea again!) But more importantly, you can start seeing opportunities to position yourself with greater clarity and purpose. Can you fulfill employers' needs? Do you align with a dean's external stakeholder priorities? Does your story match the school's current narrative? We'll get into all that much more in part II: The Art and Science of Standing Out.

In short, it's not just your career that is of concern in this process. It's the ecosystem's multiple agendas.

YOUR STRATEGIC SWOT

What assumptions have I been making about who decides admissions outcomes, and how does the real story apply to me?

Which internal stakeholders (faculty, deans, career services) might value my background, and which might see it as risky or not an obvious fit?

Are there external stakeholders (alumni, employers) who could provide me with additional insight that would help me in the admissions journey?

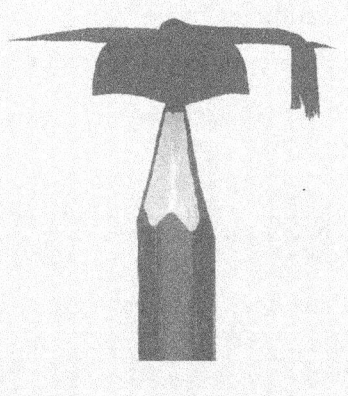

CHAPTER 3

How Decisions Really Get Made

How do MBA admissions decisions get made? That's the million-dollar question. Or, more precisely, the quarter-million-dollar question! Twenty-two of the top twenty-five MBA programs in the US now charge more than $100,000 in tuition per year, and the five most expensive programs cost more than $250,000 in total.[30] And yet, long before anyone makes the first tuition payment, the real questions on every applicant's mind are, Which program is going to invest in *me*? Will they decide to offer me a space in their next class, or will I get the dreaded log-in prompt that leads to a polite but unmistakable no?

Yes, admissions is ultimately a mutual investment decision. Applicants often think only in terms of the investment they'll be making to earn an MBA degree—time, money, opportunity cost. But it's important to realize that schools are investing, too. By offering you a spot, they're committing the time of highly paid

---

30 Marc Ethier, "What It Costs to Get an MBA from a Top Business School," *Poets & Quants*, August 28, 2024, https://poetsandquants.com/2024/08/28/what-it-costs-to-get-an-mba-from-a-top-business-school/.

faculty, the support of career services and alumni networks, and the weight of their reputation.

In part II of this book, we'll get into the strategies applicants can use to prove they are worthy of that investment the schools will make. But to have a foundation on which to base those strategies, it's important to understand how admissions decisions are actually made. So, in this chapter, we'll look at what factors into the decisions and what's going on behind the scenes in the admissions office, starting with some basics of the process, then examining what they're really looking for, and finally, exploring the more nuanced elements that inevitably arise when a group of human beings tries to make collective, high-stakes decisions.

You've learned already about the perspective each stakeholder brings when influencing decisions; now, let's step into the room, figuratively, and see how those perspectives come together (or collide) when applications are on the table and decisions have to be made.

The Rhythm of MBA Admissions: Cycles and Rounds

Each MBA admissions cycle typically begins in the summer, when applications open for the next academic year. Schools announce that the "2026–2027 admissions cycle is live," for example, and deadlines roll out across several months. Admissions cycles stretch from the date applications open to the finalizing of the class. The cycle is typically about a ten- to twelve-month process of reviewing applications and making offers (and issuing rejections and waiting list spots). A cycle usually starts in summer and ends by early summer of the following year, with wait-list activity sometimes spilling into the next cycle.

Within a cycle, most US business schools offer three rounds, though some offer a fourth or use rolling admissions instead. Here's how the timing usually works:

- **Round 1:** Application deadlines are typically in September or October.

- **Round 2:** Deadlines usually fall in early January.

- **Round 3:** Deadlines are in March or April.

Some programs may introduce additional rounds if needed, which can be a sign that their prior rounds didn't meet enrollment goals. Or they might be responding to an extraordinary event such as a global pandemic.

International programs, particularly in Europe, tend to offer more rounds and greater flexibility. Four or more rounds is common, and some schools keep reviewing applications later into the spring or even early summer. For example, INSEAD, which has campuses in France and Singapore, typically offers four rounds with deadlines from September to March. LBS offers five rounds, giving applicants a wider time horizon.

What Happens After Applicants Hit Submit

The review process can vary from school to school depending on factors such as the volume of applications and the size and composition of the admissions team. Still, there are common stages that most applications move through on the way to a final decision.

First, the application undergoes a completion check. Admissions staff verify that all required elements—transcripts, test scores, essays, résumé, and recommendations—are in place. They often do this with the help of automated features embedded in application platforms that track application completion status (such as Slate, which you can read about at https://technolutions.com/). Even one missing item, such as a pending recommendation letter or official transcripts, can delay or prevent an application from entering the review queue, although the application can still move forward.

In the past, I have seen examples where the file may then go through an initial automated screening to check for applicants who fall below certain benchmarks for GPA, GMAT, or GRE score, or years of experience.

From there, the application is typically routed to a human reader, often an admissions officer or trained reviewer. Schools with high volumes even employ temporary, seasonal readers to help get through this early stage. For example, I was a seasonal reader at the Johns Hopkins University School of Advanced International Studies, where I evaluated applications for the dual degree Master of Arts in International Relations and MBA with INSEAD, Wharton, Tuck, and Darden.

The reader assesses academic credentials, career trajectory and goals, evidence of leadership, and how well the applicant's values align with the program's culture. Many schools use an internal rubric to score these attributes for consistency across readers, and most schools ensure that each application gets read by at least two people to minimize bias.

PRO TIP: REMEMBER THE HUMAN

Don't forget that *human* is a keyword in *human reader*. Before your application goes to committee, it might first be reviewed by someone scrolling through it from their home office with a Starbucks Caramel Frappuccino on their desk. Admissions officers are real people, with kids to pick up from daycare, inboxes overflowing, and maybe a dog barking in the background. They have a job to do amid all that, and *your* job is to make theirs easier by presenting a clear, compelling application that helps them say yes. (More on how to do that in part II.)

From the initial read, an applicant might be invited to an interview, which signals serious consideration but is not a guarantee of admission. Anecdotally speaking, I've seen 40 to 50 percent acceptance rates after interviews. Depending on the school, the interview might be with a second-year student, alumni, admissions officers, or even faculty. This stage provides insight into applicants' communication skills, professional polish, and cultural fit. Remember, they need to assess how you will communicate in the classroom. One M7 school is inviting more people to interview than in the past because they find one part of the interview to be a better predictor of success in the program than test scores and other metrics. As I tell my clients, business schools can't admit you, try you out, and then send you home if you don't live up to their expectations! The interviewers' notes are added to the file and factored into the final decision.

Finally, the file enters committee review. A group of admissions professionals convenes to discuss each applicant against broader enrollment goals. These include constructing a well-rounded class across industries, geographies, backgrounds, and post-MBA interests. The committee makes the final admit, wait-list, or deny decisions, sometimes after much discussion when there isn't an immediate consensus.

Numbers and Nuance Behind Decisions

Some perplexing contradictions happen in MBA admissions that have both applicants and independent admissions consultants alike scratching their heads. Every year, hundreds of candidates with sky-high test scores and near-perfect grades are rejected from top business schools. And every year, many applicants are accepted with scores well below the median.

Even the most elite MBA programs admit students with a wide range of GMAT scores. For example, Yale SOM class of 2027 had GMAT Focus scores ranging from 638 to 715.[31]

This really isn't so perplexing, however, and it makes perfect sense when you think about business schools' commitment to holistic admissions decisions. Admissions committees typically evaluate applications across both quantitative and qualitative dimensions. On the objective side, GMAT/GRE scores and undergraduate GPA *are* key indicators of academic preparedness, but the combined qualitative inputs, such as essays, interviews, recommendations, and leadership experience, also influence decision-making and can even outweigh raw test numbers. So, a lower-than-median score does not automatically disqualify an applicant.

Admissions officers also factor in professional maturity, the caliber of work experience, fit with school values, and the unique cultural background and worldview of each applicant. Even components such as international study, work, or travel experience and extracurricular

---

31   "Class Profile: Class of 2027," Yale School of Management, https://som.yale.edu/
        programs/mba/admissions/class-profile.

engagement play a role when schools seek to shape a globally astute and community-minded incoming class.

The nuance of admissions decisions comes into play when you zoom out to remember what was covered in chapters 1 and 2 regarding the macro influences on admissions decisions. Admissions officers are not simply evaluating one applicant to select the best individuals in a vacuum. They are shaping a class. Schools seek diversity of life experiences, industry backgrounds and career goals, geography, and identity. You can be an incredibly competitive applicant and still not get in because the program already has three other people like you. Admissions teams are more like architects than evaluators. In fact, an M7 admissions officer shared, "It's about what the institution needs, not whom I like."

The Psychology of Admissions Decisions

Even with all the logic, structure, and rigor that admissions offices bring to the application review process, there remains an undeniable wild card: psychology. While most decisions follow a structured protocol, with clear steps from review to committee, human and organizational behavior can be at play. I've heard from colleagues of so many instances in which an application seemed like a certainty but didn't get through committee review, while others that seemed like long shots surprisingly earned a spot. One of my favorite stories is of a client who was shocked to get accepted by Yale SOM. His enthusiastic email to me was succinct: "Didn't see that one coming!"

Below are some of the most common psychological dynamics that can influence decision-making.

NOISE AND BIAS

Cognitive neuroscience has shown that even highly trained professionals vary in their judgments because of mental fatigue, mood, order effects, and social dynamics. For example, in their book *Noise*, Daniel Kahneman, Olivier Sibony, and Cass R. Sunstein describe those factors as the unwanted variability in professional judgment and clarify that noise is distinct from bias. Bias happens when decisions consistently lean in one direction, such as being too strict or too lenient. Noise, by contrast, is inconsistency: The same application might be rated very differently depending on who reads it, when they read it, and what else they've seen that day.[32]

GROUPTHINK

Groupthink happens when a cohesive team prioritizes harmony over critical evaluation. A senior admissions officer's strong opinion, or a junior admissions representative who is particularly persuasive, can steer the entire room, sometimes silencing disagreement before it can surface.

GROUP POLARIZATION

When committee members share views, discussion often moves the group to a more extreme position. An enthusiastic advocate, or a sharp critic, can set the tone, resulting in decisions more polarized than any one member's original stance.

---

32   Daniel Kahneman et al., *Noise: A Flaw in Human Judgment* (Little, Brown Spark, 2021).

CONFORMITY PRESSURE

The urge to fit in, especially in a hierarchical group, can lead individuals to suppress dissent. Junior staff or new reviewers might remain silent, even if they see merit (or red flags) in an application.

THE ABILENE PARADOX

Groups can reject a candidate not because anyone objects but because no one realizes others see potential. Without an advocate, a qualified applicant can be overlooked because of mistaken assumptions about the group's preferences.

DIFFUSION OF RESPONSIBILITY

When multiple people share decision-making, individuals may assume someone else will speak up. This diffusion can lead to inaction, especially for the unconventional applicant who needs a champion.

DECISION FATIGUE

After making many decisions in succession, the brain tires. As cognitive resources dwindle, people rely more on simple rules or defaults. In admissions, this could show up as a tendency to reject borderline files late in the reading day, when mental energy is low.[33]

Pointing out that these factors could possibly be at work, some of the time, in MBA admissions is *not* a critique of the integrity of admissions professionals but instead is an evidence-backed recognition of the human condition. Even with good systems and noble intentions, admissions teams operate under pressure, deadlines, and ambiguity.

---

33   A. Taylor et al., "Decision Fatigue in Professional Judgment: A Systematic Review," *Health Psychology Review* 19, no. 2 (2025): 144–67.

They are human beings, and nothing you can say in your application or do in your interview can change that!

Your Bottom Line

You can't control institutional priorities or the shifts in applicant pools each cycle, but you will feel more empowered in the applicant journey if you understand the environment in which those decisions get made.

The more you internalize that this process is about context, not just credentials, the faster you can bounce back from setbacks, such as by not taking rejection personally (which you'll hear more about in chapter 7), and the more clearly you'll see the path to position yourself strategically in the chapters to come.

YOUR STRATEGIC SWOT

What do you offer that conveys your unique value to a cohort?

Where might a committee perceive risk or redundancy in your profile?

What external or institutional pressures at the time of your application could complicate your candidacy, and how can you counter them?

How can the psychology of admissions decisions provide you with new insight that empowers you in the application journey?

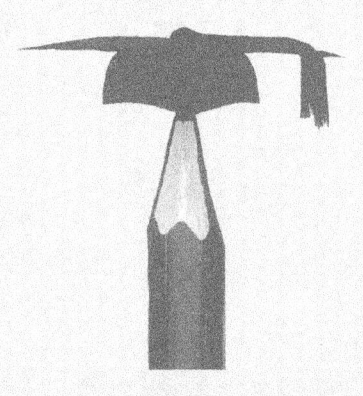

PART II

The Art and Science of Standing Out

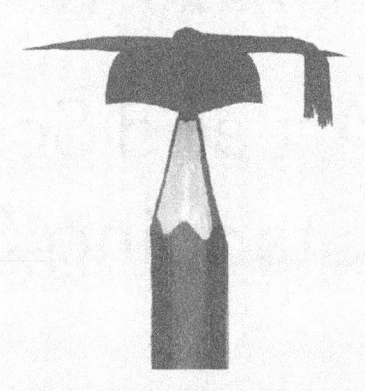

CHAPTER 4

Position Yourself for Success

What we know matters, but who we are matters more.[34]

—BRENÉ BROWN, PROFESSOR OF PRACTICE
IN MANAGEMENT, UNIVERSITY OF TEXAS AT
AUSTIN MCCOMBS SCHOOL OF BUSINESS

A s a prominent researcher and best-selling author, Brené Brown's thought leadership on courage and vulnerability should resonate well beyond corporate boardrooms to anyone embarking on the MBA admissions journey. The admissions office needs to understand who you are, not just what you know, and conveying who you are often means demonstrating courage and vulnerability.

This section of the book begins not with the mechanics of applications but with positioning yourself for success by examining who you are and what you want. This chapter is about clarifying your goals,

---

34   Brené Brown, *Daring Greatly: How the Courage to Be Vulnerable Transforms the Way We Live, Love, Parent, and Lead* (Gotham Books, 2012), 16.

identifying the value you bring, and strengthening the narrative that will carry through the application.

Later, when you are awash in timelines and checklists, this groundwork will keep you from treating the process as a series of disconnected tasks, with each one feeling like you're having to start from scratch. Instead, you will approach the application process with a cohesive, integrated sense of intention, confidence, purpose, and alignment between what you know and who you are.

Overwhelm Is Normal

First, let's address the biggest barrier that can get in the way of positioning you for success: feeling overwhelmed. Whether you are at the very beginning stage of considering applying or are knee-deep in essays and interview preparation, some stress is natural and perfectly fine. It means that you're taking the process seriously—you understand that applying for an MBA is a big deal. High stakes and uncertainty naturally produce anxiety, but it's important to keep your stress level in check so that you don't throw in the towel and not even apply.

We'll go more into managing those emotions in chapter 6, The Psychology of Applications, because they can show up at every stage of the journey, from the moment you decide to apply to the day you choose which offer to accept. For now, know that the preparation you'll do in this chapter can actually help reduce that stress. By stepping back to clarify why you want an MBA, what you offer a program, and how you'll present yourself, you create a road map. That clarity makes the next stage, tackling the application itself, less daunting because you'll be moving forward with intention instead of reacting in the moment.

Begin with Self-Awareness

It all starts with self-awareness. Before choosing where to apply and crafting a compelling story for your applications, you need to know the raw material you're working with. This includes your values, motivations, strengths, weaknesses, and the life experiences that have shaped you. This foundation will guide every decision you make, from the schools you target to the examples you choose to talk about in essays and interviews.

CLARIFY YOUR GOALS AND MOTIVATIONS

The first question to ask yourself is, *Why do I want an MBA?* Are you looking to accelerate a career trajectory already in motion? Pivot into a new industry or function? Gain global exposure or strengthen leadership skills? Start a new venture? Build a network that could change your life? Do you have some other reasons?

Avoid labeling your reasons "good" or "bad." This is not a time to be judgmental toward yourself. (And please don't let anyone else try to tell you that your reasons for wanting to go are good or bad.) Instead, think in terms of *surface* reasons (prestige, salary increase) versus *core* reasons (leading large-scale change, solving complex problems, creating social impact). Both can be valid, but self-awareness means recognizing which matters most to you and why. If you can't explain your own motivations to yourself, you won't be able to explain them convincingly to an admissions committee.

The key here is to put real thought into why you want to go so that your intentions and commitment will shine through in your application. When I worked in admissions, a colleague who reviewed part-time MBA applications was always amazed at what were clearly last-minute, impulsive submissions before the application deadline.

She would shake her head and say, "It's as if they wake up on Saturday morning thinking, *I should go to the grocery store today, drop off shirts at the dry cleaner, and, oh yeah, apply for an MBA.*"

It's perfectly fine if the idea does strike you out of the blue on a random weekend. The plan to go to business school does not have to have been brewing for years for you to be a strong applicant. But once it comes to you, give yourself the gift of pausing to reflect on your reasons. That clarity will make the rest of the application process far smoother and your candidacy stronger.

KNOW THE ENVIRONMENT WHERE YOU THRIVE

Every business school has its own personality—urban versus rural, competitive versus collaborative, traditional versus innovative, and so on. The environment and culture of a program can shape your experience just as much as the curriculum. A campus in a major city may surround you with constant professional events and industry meetups. A suburban or rural location might foster deeper connections with classmates because everyone's social life is centered on campus.

You might also find two programs in similar settings but with very different classroom experiences. Some are steeped in the classic case-study method, while others feature more hands-on consulting projects or other experiential learning opportunities. Neither is inherently better, but one might be a better match for your learning style, personality, and goals.

When we talk about a program's environment, we're talking about the full package of factors that shape day-to-day experience.

- **Physical location:** urban, suburban, or rural setting; climate; cost of living; proximity to industry hubs

- **Campus footprint:** a single main campus versus multiple campuses across regions or countries

- **Culture:** competitive versus collaborative, formal versus informal, socially active versus more reserved

- **Program structure:** pace and intensity, schedule flexibility, and the style of curriculum delivery (in-person, online, or hybrid options)

- **Class composition:** size of the cohort, diversity of backgrounds and nationalities, range of industries represented

- **Extracurricular ecosystem:** availability of clubs, conferences, competitions, and social events

- **Networking environment:** opportunities for interaction with alumni, industry leaders, and recruiters

When you're thinking about where you'll thrive, ask yourself some of these questions:

- Do I want to be in the heart of a business hub, or would I prefer a quieter setting where the focus is entirely on the program?

- How much do climate, cost of living, and local culture matter to me?

- Do I want a cohort that's large enough to have multiple niche groups or small enough that I'll know everyone by name? Some programs are large enough that you can be somewhat anonymous, whereas at others, you'll find yourself not able to walk across campus without familiar faces asking you how your day is going!

- Looking back at my undergraduate experience, which aspects of that environment worked for me or didn't? Was it large or small, public or private? Was it rooted in certain values? Do I want to replicate that or choose something different this time?

- What have I learned from past work environments about the size of the organization, the nature of the team, and the culture I function best in? Since MBA programs involve collaborating on real-world projects, those same dynamics will come into play.

Take the time to picture your daily life in the program—where you'll live, how you'll spend your time outside of class, and who you'll be surrounded by. The better the fit, the more likely you are to bring your full self to the experience and to get the most out of it.

TAKE AN HONEST LOOK AT STRENGTHS AND WEAKNESSES

Self-awareness also means facing the reality of your candidacy, and that reality has two sides. First, there's the way you'll handle the process itself, including the logistics of researching programs, meeting deadlines, preparing essays, managing interviews, and making decisions once responses come in. Second, there's your strength as an applicant—how competitive you are for the schools on your list, given your profile. Both deserve an honest assessment before you dive in.

Strengths and Weaknesses for the Application Process

The MBA application process is a project in itself. Some people thrive on timelines, checklists, and multiple moving parts; others find them overwhelming. You may be confident about writing polished essays but dread interviews. Or perhaps you're confident about interviewing but need help telling your story in writing. If you know in advance where you're likely to get tripped up, you can plan for it by building in extra time, enlisting help, or seeking out resources.

The same goes for decision-making. Some applicants freeze when they get multiple offers; others love negotiating and see it as an opportunity to ask for more scholarship money. Knowing your process strengths and weaknesses gives you the power to stay in control rather than letting the process control you.

 ## PRO TIP: INTERVIEW YOURSELF FOR BUSINESS SCHOOL

Consider asking yourself these questions to assess your strengths and weaknesses around the process of applying to business school:

- How comfortable am I managing multiple deadlines and application components at once?
- Do I tend to procrastinate, or do I start early and pace myself well?
- Which parts of the process (research, writing, interviews) energize me, and which drain me?
- How do I typically make big decisions under pressure?

Once you've identified your process gaps, think about where to get support. That might be a friend, trusted colleague, or admissions consultant. I've even had clients who asked their therapist for advice on answering the "What Matters Most to You, and Why" essay for GSB. The right help at the right time can turn a stumbling block into a strength.

Strengths and Weaknesses in Your Candidacy

This is the part most applicants think of first: How strong am I for the schools I'm targeting? Assessing that is not as straightforward as it sounds. It's one thing to look at hard data—your test scores, GPA, quantitative skills, or résumé accomplishments. It's another to step back and evaluate the less tangible aspects of your candidacy, such as whether your career path shows a distinctive trajectory, whether your industry experience is over- or underrepresented in the applicant pool, or whether your background and life experiences will stand out to a committee.

Some applicants worry that they lack the wow factor. Maybe their demographic profile is too basic in the MBA world, or their career path feels conventional compared to peers who have launched start-ups or worked in unusual niche industries. Others underestimate how compelling their everyday experiences will sound.

To uncover the "hidden gems" in your life story, or to think more fully about the obvious highlights (and lowlights) of your life, take stock of significant experiences that have shaped you, both personally and professionally. These might include challenges you've overcome, achievements you're proud of, pivotal career decisions, or formative life events outside of work or school. Looking at your life as a whole can reveal themes that connect seemingly unrelated experiences and may strengthen your application story.

As you review both the quantitative and qualitative data of your life, keep in mind that judging one's own abilities and distinctiveness accurately is harder than most realize. In one seminal study, people in the lowest quartile of performance consistently rated themselves far above average, a pattern known as the Dunning–

Kruger effect.[35] Other research has found that men are more likely to overestimate their abilities, while women tend to underestimate theirs, even when actual performance is the same.[36] These patterns start surprisingly early: In school experiments, young boys often overrate their abilities and negotiate more for rewards than girls, despite equivalent results.[37]

I can't count how many clients have asked, with serious doubt in their voices, "Do you think I'm Harvard material?" "Do you think I have any chance getting into Wharton?" and then have gone on to get into schools they assumed were out of reach (with great scholarships too!). Sometimes, we underestimate ourselves or are held back by people in the past who misjudged our potential. This process can conjure up the voice of that middle school teacher who made you feel like you weren't going to amount to anything or the high school counselor who said you'd never get into an Ivy League school. Other times, we need to face the fact that it would be easier to win the Mega Millions lottery than get accepted to a program with a single-digit acceptance rate. The point isn't to talk yourself out of aiming high; it's to understand where you stand so you can highlight your advantages, shore up weaknesses, and put together a strategy that gives you the best shot.

---

35   Justin Kruger and David Dunning, "Unskilled and Unaware of It: How Difficulties in Recognizing One's Own Incompetence Lead to Inflated Self-Assessments," *Journal of Personality and Social Psychology* 77, no. 6 (1999): 1121–34.

36   Sylvain Bodard et al., "Impact of Gender on Self-Assessment Accuracy Among Fourth-Year French Medical Students on Faculty's Online Objective Structured Clinical Examinations," *BMC Medical Education*, no. 1553 (2024), https://doi.org/10.1186/s12909-024-06573-x.

37   Stephanie Arnold et al., "Study Finds Gender Gap with Children When It Comes to Negotiating," *NYU News*, January 16, 2025.

PRO TIP: INTERVIEW YOURSELF FOR AN MBA

Ask yourself these questions to assess the strengths and weaknesses of your candidacy for MBA programs:

- Which elements of my profile are likely to stand out?
- Where might admissions readers have concerns, and how can I address them?
- How do my stats (test scores, GPA) compare with the schools' class profiles?
- What unique experiences or perspectives can I offer that nobody else can?
- What patterns do I see in my career, academic, and personal choices?
- What moments am I most proud of, and why?
- Which experiences best illustrate resilience or adaptability?
- How have I demonstrated intentionality and impact in my professional life?
- If there are six other candidates competing for a seat, why should it be me?

Once you've mapped your candidacy strengths and weaknesses, consider who or what can help you close the gaps before you are ready to submit. This could be skill-building courses, leadership opportunities, or extracurricular activities that boost your profile. Even small, well-chosen steps can make a meaningful difference in optimizing your chances for admission.

Leadership: More than a Title

Business schools see themselves as leadership incubators. They're in the business of developing leaders or building stronger, more effective ones if you arrive with leadership experience. That's why they look for evidence that you either have strong leadership potential or the capacity to grow well beyond the leader you are today.

Part of positioning yourself for success means understanding who you are as a leader right now, what kind of leadership you want to grow into, and what evidence you can point to that demonstrates your leadership capabilities.

The good news is that there's no single mold you have to fit. Leadership can be defined in many ways, and realizing this can be freeing. Management scholar Warren Bennis, who served on the faculty at MIT Sloan School of Management, describes leadership as "the capacity to translate vision into reality" and emphasizes that it begins with self-awareness—knowing who you are and staying true to that identity as you step forward.[38] In his book *Good to Great*, Jim Collins, who has an MBA from Stanford, paints a different but complementary picture with his "Level 5 leadership," which is a paradoxical blend of personal humility and fierce resolve that moves organizations from good to exceptional.[39]

These perspectives share a common thread: Leadership isn't earned solely through titles, résumés, or formal authority. It emerges when you act on your vision, inspire others toward a shared goal, and maintain the resolve to see something through. For some applicants, that might mean steering a work team through a crisis; for others, organizing a volunteer initiative, mentoring a peer, or pioneering a

---

38   Warren Bennis, *On Becoming a Leader*, 4th ed. (Basic Books, 2009), 41.

39   Jim Collins, "Level 5 Leadership," Jim Collins, https://www.jimcollins.com/concepts/level-five-leadership.html.

process improvement. What matters is that you recognize your leadership moments, whatever their scale or setting, and can articulate how they have shaped you and the kind of leader you are becoming.

DRAW ON MULTIPLE SOURCES FOR INSIGHT

Beyond the reflection questions provided earlier in this self-awareness section, you may want to turn to additional sources beyond what you know about yourself off the top of your head. These can provide new perspectives, confirm patterns you've already noticed, and sometimes uncover blind spots you didn't know you had.

Past Feedback

Review feedback you've received in performance reviews, letters of recommendation, or informal conversations with managers, professors, or peers. Pay attention to recurring themes, whether they're about your communication skills, leadership style, problem-solving ability, or areas for improvement.

Formal Assessments

Consider taking formal personality, strengths, or work style assessments. Tools such as the CliftonStrengths assessment, Hogan Assessments, the Myers–Briggs Type Indicator, or the DiSC assessment can help you better understand how you operate, what motivates you, and how you interact with others. These might be offered through your employer, your alma mater's alumni career services office, or independent career counselors and career coaches (who can be found through the National Career Development Association in the "Looking for Career Help" section at www.ncda.org). While no single assessment will capture everything about you, the insights can add depth to your self-awareness and help you frame your strengths and growth areas in the application process.

Adding input from other sources such as formal assessments or others' feedback ensures you're not relying solely on memory or self-perception, which can sometimes be incomplete or biased. The more angles you use to understand yourself, the clearer your picture will be and the better equipped you'll be to position yourself for MBA admissions success.

From Self-Awareness to Story

Everything we've just covered—examining your goals, preferred environment, strengths and weaknesses, life experiences, and leadership style—forms the raw material for your MBA story. I hope you see that self-awareness isn't about ticking boxes on a questionnaire or glancing over your résumé; it's about understanding yourself well enough to choose which threads to weave together to form a picture of who you are and what you have to offer.

The clearer you are about who you are, what you want, and how you operate, the easier it will be to craft a story that feels authentic to you, captures what's distinctive about your candidacy, and resonates with the people deciding your future. This leads us to focusing on your story.

THE STRATEGY BEHIND YOUR STORY

When I talk about your story in terms of MBA applications, I don't just mean the facts of your résumé, your transcript, or a list of achievements. You are so much more than that. You're an amalgam of life experiences, perspectives, successes and disappointments, progress and setbacks, joys and tragedies, all of which can move the admissions team to want to know more about you or to want you to join them where they are.

Stanford business professor Jennifer Aaker defines *story* as "a connected series of events with a beginning, a middle, and an end, and it's a journey that moves the listener.[40] So, as you begin your application, it's important to take your self-awareness and shape it into a story that takes the admissions team on a journey. This will not only differentiate you from your competitors—after all, no one else has lived the story you have to tell—but will also make the application process easier. From your essays to your résumé, recommendation letters, and interviews, your story will provide the context and content that guide what you say and how you say it.

In chapter 5, we'll get into more detail about how your story plays out in various aspects of your applications, particularly in essays. But here, the key is to begin shaping the story that will position you for success.

BUT I THOUGHT IT'S NOT ABOUT ME!

With the focus shifting to you and your story, you might be thinking, *Wait—now you're telling me to focus on my story? Isn't that the opposite of "It's not about you"?* Sure, your story is very much about you—your experiences, values, and what makes you who you are. That's what makes it authentic and memorable. But in the context of MBA admissions, your story isn't *for* you. It's for the people making the decision to obtain a clear picture of how you will contribute to their program's goals, culture, and community. So, it's as much about them as it is about you.

---

40 Jennifer Aaker, "Harnessing the Power of Stories," Stanford VMware Women's Leadership Lab, https://womensleadership.stanford.edu/node/796/harnessing-power-stories.

Your story is a persuasion tool. Aaker describes it this way: "When a listener goes on that journey, they feel different, and the result is persuasion, and sometimes action."[41] So, what I hope you will remember throughout your application process is that when crafted strategically and told compellingly, your story can persuade admissions representatives to take the action you hope for: accepting you into their MBA program! When you tell an engaging story with a distinct through line rather than just presenting yourself as a collection of disparate data points, you are helping them make a more informed decision about your candidacy.[42]

To do that well, you need to understand your story on two levels—the big-picture essence of who you are and the concrete way you bring that essence to life.

STORY IS BOTH ABSTRACT AND CONCRETE

When I talk about your story, I mean it in two different but connected ways. First, there's the abstract level—the big-picture essence of who you are. This is the collection of qualities, experiences, values, and motivations that define you. It's your personal brand, your unique value proposition, or simply the "golden thread" that explains why you've made the choices you've made, how those experiences have shaped who you are, and how they've created the value you'll bring to an MBA program.

Then there's the concrete level—how that essence takes shape in the actual telling. This is the narrative itself: the words you choose, the details you highlight or leave out, the sequence and arc you create, and the tone you set. In your application essays, you are putting that story into writing; in admissions interviews, you bring

---

41   Ibid.

42   Ibid.

it to life in conversation. Both levels matter; the abstract provides the substance, and the concrete delivers it in a way that resonates with the reader or listener.

PRO TIP: REMEMBER THE EMOTIONAL POWER OF STORIES

As you craft your story, keep in mind that stories don't just entertain; they work on us at a primal level. Our brains are wired to seek meaning through narrative. This instinctual part of the brain, sometimes called the lizard brain, is attuned to patterns, conflict, and resolution because those elements once helped us survive. When a story unfolds, it sparks emotional and sensory areas of the brain, creating anticipation and activating memory systems in ways that bullet points and statistics can't. That's why stories make abstract qualities such as leadership or resilience feel concrete and relatable and why a well-told story can linger long after the facts have faded.[43]

STRATEGY: SHAPING YOUR STORY WITH INTENTION

Admissions committees are assessing what they can't get from another candidate: the particular mix of experience, perspective, and character that sets you apart. Shaping your strategy means asking yourself key questions before you draft an essay or sit for an interview.

---

43   Will Storr, *The Science of Storytelling: Why Stories Make Us Human, and How to Tell Them Better* (Abrams Press, 2020).

- Which personal, professional, and educational experiences have shaped me the most?

- What patterns or themes emerge from my successes, challenges, and turning points?

- What did I learn about myself through these experiences?

- Which of these align best with the values of my target programs?

- Where are the gaps or weaknesses in my profile, and how can I address them without being defensive?

The answers will help you decide what to emphasize, what to omit, and how to tell a consistent story across every part of your application. Think about what is rare in your story and make sure to emphasize that, while not diluting your story with distracting information. This ensures the committee won't miss what's important and will recognize your uniqueness.

For example, one client of mine left her job to care for her father while her mother was living with dementia. This was a life choice that created a gap in her résumé, but instead of that coming across as a professional liability, she positioned it as an experience that taught her empathy, adaptability, and resilience in difficult circumstances. Those qualities would enrich her MBA cohort in their leadership development just as much as the technical skills or professional accolades she brought into the classroom.

PRO TIP: MAKE YOURSELF SCARCE

The scarcity principle is a core idea in persuasion science. It suggests that people value what appears limited or hard to obtain. Think about what makes you different and how you can communicate that. When you use this principle ethically in the application process, your story can reflect distinctive traits that admissions committees genuinely can't get from another applicant.[44]

CONSISTENCY IS COMPELLING

The most compelling stories are the ones that ring true across all aspects of your application. That means that the themes you emphasize in your essays are backed up by what others say about you in recommendations, by the evidence provided in your résumé, and through the way you speak about yourself in an interview. When I worked in admissions, my boss, a professor of marketing and the director of postgraduate programs, would even write the word *consistent* on an evaluation sheet when an applicant's essays, résumé, and recommendations all reinforced the same themes.

One client of mine accepted at a top two program in Europe illustrated this perfectly. He worked in strategy and development for a medical device company that had been acquired, which first exposed him to the world of entrepreneurship through acquisition (ETA). He decided that after an MBA, his goal was to raise a search fund and acquire, operate, and scale a medical device healthcare company of his own. Although he hadn't yet worked in ETA, every element of his

---

44   Christopher Cannon et al., *Understanding Scarcity: From Marketing to Policy, Management, and Beyond* (Now Publishers, 2024).

application painted a consistent picture of his readiness to pursue that path. His essays told the story of how his career experiences equipped him with the skills and knowledge needed for ETA. His résumé documented concrete achievements in strategy and development. And his manager wrote a powerful recommendation letter highlighting exactly those qualities that would make him a strong operator and future leader and also verifying that he had been exposed to a complex acquisition. Taken together, the application's components presented a compelling coherence.

AUTHENTICITY: LEADING WITH THE TRUTH

These days, the word *authenticity* gets thrown around so much that it's in danger of becoming just another buzzword, especially in business, leadership, and even MBA admissions. If I'm asking you to be authentic in how you tell your story, it seems only fair that I should define it rather than just tossing the term out there!

So, what does *authenticity* really mean?

The concept has early roots in humanistic psychology, with Carl Rogers, who taught at the University of Chicago, defining authenticity as being genuine, having your outward behavior line up with your inner experience.[45] HBS Professor Bill George describes authentic leaders as "genuine people who are true to themselves and to what they believe in. They engender trust and develop genuine connections with others." And goes on to say that "your life story defines your leadership."[46] Herminia Ibarra, an INSEAD professor, points out that authenticity evolves as we grow into new roles, emphasizing that effective leaders experiment, stretch, and adapt rather than staying

---

45   Carl R. Rogers, *On Becoming a Person: A Therapist's View of Psychotherapy*, 2nd ed. (Houghton Mifflin, 1995).

46   Bill George, *True North: Discover Your Authentic Leadership* (Jossey-Bass, 2007), xxxi, 8.

locked into a fixed idea of themselves.[47] There's a cautionary tale in all this, though. Adam Grant, a well-known Wharton professor and one of the world's most influential management thinkers, cautions that "be yourself" can be taken too literally and can backfire if it leads to unfiltered oversharing.[48]

This is all easier said than done, of course, and applicants often worry about blowing their chances if they are too open. While each situation has to be evaluated on a case-by-case basis against your overall application profile and the culture of where you're applying, I can tell you that generally, MBA application strategy is not about an episode of the *Call Her Daddy* podcast but is about choosing to tell the truth about what matters most, in a way that demonstrates self-awareness, growth, and who you are (or could become) as a leader.

This was thoughtfully done by an applicant to M7 schools who made the choice to tell a story that presented her in an unflattering light, as it revealed her reaction and true feelings when a close family member went through a difficult experience. While many applicants would be afraid to disclose something that felt shameful, she chose to talk about her own capacity for self-reflection, empathy, and growth. She not only was accepted to a top three M7 program but was also the recipient of a scholarship.

FIT: MAKING IT CLEAR YOU BELONG THERE

Even the most authentic, well-crafted story won't result in an offer of admission if the committee can't see how you'll thrive in their program. Fit is about connecting your unique story to the school's

---

47   Herminia Ibarra, "The Authenticity Paradox," *Harvard Business Review* 93, no. 1/2 (2015): 53–59.

48   Adam Grant, "Unless You're Oprah, 'Be Yourself' Is Terrible Advice," *The New York Times*, June 4, 2016, https://www.nytimes.com/2016/06/05/opinion/sunday/unless-youre-oprah-be-yourself-is-terrible-advice.html.

mission, culture, and goals, showing not just why you want them but how they would benefit from having you in the program.

This doesn't mean repeating the school's marketing language. And it doesn't mean contradicting what I've just said about authenticity. You can still be true to yourself while showing them why you would be a great addition to the cohort. Fit means demonstrating, through the themes in your story, that you understand what the program values and how you'll contribute.

Admissions officers are not just gatekeepers; they are kind people who feel bad about denying admission to deserving applicants. I've heard them confess that they sometimes lose sleep over it. They are human, and they do second-guess themselves! But most of all, they want to give each seat to a person who will succeed in the program and make the most of the experience. And they are constrained by not having enough seats for every qualified applicant.

 ## PRO TIP: FLIP THE SCRIPT

Put yourself in the shoes of the admissions readers. Pretend *you* are the head of the admissions department, with or without your Starbucks on your desk. Imagine reading your application from their perspective. Why should they accept you? If they say yes to you, that means they are saying no to someone else.

Your Bottom Line

Positioning yourself for MBA admissions success starts long before you upload a transcript or draft an essay. It means reflecting on who you are, what you want, and how you operate at your best.

It means clarifying your goals, assessing the environments where you'll thrive, taking a clear-eyed look at your strengths and weaknesses—both in handling the process and in the strength of your candidacy—and then shaping all of that into a story that's both authentic and strategic.

When you can articulate your value with clarity, connect it to what your target programs seek, and demonstrate genuine fit, you transform from being one of many qualified applicants to the one they must have in the class.

YOUR STRATEGIC SWOT

- Which qualities, experiences, or achievements are most powerful, and how can I highlight them consistently across my application?

- Which gaps in my candidacy (skills, experiences, stats, or perceived fit) could show up as red flags in my application, and how might I address them before applying?

- Where in the application process itself am I most likely to struggle—research, writing, deadlines, interviews, etc.—and how can I proactively get support?

- What upcoming experiences, projects, or roles could strengthen my profile if I seek them out now?

- Which relationships, mentors, or networks could help me better understand my fit for specific programs or provide insight into how my story will be received?

CHAPTER 5

Your Application Strategy

At its core, applying to business school is a series of decisions. Which schools should I apply to? Should I retake the GMAT for a better score? Should my essay focus on a personal or professional experience? This mirrors the decision-making process of effective business leaders who gather input from many sources, study the data, convene team discussions, and maybe even bring in outside consultants to provide expertise. They listen carefully, weigh different perspectives, and consider the risks and rewards of each option. But at the end of the day, strong leaders know that the responsibility ultimately rests with them.

Applying to MBA programs works the same way. From reading threads on Reddit or GMAT Club to conversing with alumni, attending official school webinars, conferring with independent admissions consultants, or even having your family members chime in, you'll receive input that can be valuable but also overwhelming and highly conflicting. The key is to remember that, like a business leader, you are in charge of your own strategy. You decide when to apply, where to apply, and how to present your story. This chapter will guide you in approaching those decisions with clarity and confidence so that the application you submit reflects not the noise of outside voices but the leadership of your own judgment.

We're building on the Position Yourself for Success reflections, strategies, and mindsets discussed in chapter 4, now applying them to your application. I'm intentionally keeping the advice in this chapter at a more strategic than tactical level. To put it directly, you don't need a book to repeat what you can find online about the nitty-gritty details of applications. Instead, my goal in this chapter is to tell you what you probably won't find online or to help you make sense of what you do find out there.

 MORE PRO TIPS

For more granular advice at a tactical level about all aspects of your application, I provide tips and tools through the blog and other resources on my website: www.mba360admissions.com.

Choose Your Round

One of the first strategic decisions you'll make is when to apply. Business schools structure their admissions in rounds, typically round 1 (R1) in the fall, round 2 (R2) after the new year, a later round 3 (R3) in the spring for many schools, and even some additional rounds beyond those. Schools save seats for later rounds, so applying in R2, R3, or beyond is not as risky as you might think, but each round does have its trade-offs.

ROUND 1

R1 can position you for the broadest set of options: more seats available, more scholarship funds on the table, and the chance to demonstrate enthusiasm early. But applying in R1 only helps if you are truly ready. If your test score isn't where it needs to be, your essays aren't coherent yet, or your recommenders are given tight turnarounds, rushing into R1 can hurt more than it helps.

ROUND 2

Waiting until R2 gives you more time to polish your materials and can be ideal if you need that longer runway. Or you can use R2 to apply to more schools if you applied in R1 but didn't get the results you wanted. This round is a strong entry point, as many schools build their classes with a substantial share of R2 admits. The caution here is that competition can be more intense if you are part of an over-represented demographic.

ROUND 3 AND BEYOND

Conventional wisdom is that R3 (and rounds beyond the third, which are less common but do exist) is too risky and should be avoided at all costs. Sure, by R3 or later, the class is just about full, scholarship dollars are largely allocated, and schools are often filling only very specific gaps regarding types of applicant profiles they're seeking to balance the cohort. Therefore, for many applicants, R3 and beyond should usually be treated as a backup rather than a primary strategy. For instance, you might want to consider applying in R3 if you were unsuccessful in previous rounds in that cycle. But if R3 or later ends up being the best (or sometimes only) option for you, then go for it. I *have* worked with successful applicants in R3, especially those with a unique value proposition who might just be what schools need to fill those gaps in the cohorts they're crafting.

Above all, what matters most is not which round you choose but whether you are applying at the right time in your life. External circumstances, particularly ones outside of your control (there's that idea of "It's not about you" again!), can throw even the best-laid plans off track. One client in private wealth management worked hard on his test prep, and so, in the weeks leading up to the GMAT, he felt really good about how he was going to do on the test. But tragic, unexpected personal losses in quick succession made it hard to focus. Rather than pushing forward at the wrong moment, he regrouped and waited until the following cycle. By then, he was steadier, more focused, and able to put forward his best case.

HOW TO DECIDE

Ultimately, the decision of which round to apply in has to align with who you are and how you like to operate. Are you a "get it done now" kind of person? Are you a "likely to have regrets and second-guess yourself if you rush it" kind of person? Would you rather work on your application in the summer when days are longer or in the winter when you're stuck inside?

You also want to be realistic about how ready you are. Consider this thought experiment: Imagine the application deadline is only a couple of days away and you have most of your application ready, such as test scores and recommendation letters. Ask yourself, How close am I to being ready? Or how quickly could I be ready? Which pieces of my application are not yet strong enough? If the answers are discouraging and the to-do list is long—tests to retake to try for a higher score, recommenders not lined up or briefed, essays still in rough draft—you should probably wait for the next round. If the gaps are minimal and you can address them with focused effort, the soonest round could be your best bet.

I've known of applicants who managed to write a very strong essay after starting only a few days before the deadline, while others methodically crafted their essay and overall application over a six-month period. Both approaches can result in admittance. My recommendation is to spend more time focusing on creating the most persuasive application rather than worrying about how to hedge your bets depending on the round.

PRO TIP: WHEN YOU DON'T REALLY HAVE A CHOICE

Sometimes the decision about which round to apply in isn't really a decision at all. Life circumstances can dictate your timing. For example, if you've suddenly been laid off, faced some other unexpected change at work, or encountered a personal shift, you may need to move quickly, meaning R2 or even R3 is your only option. On the other hand, you might need to apply in R1 if professional or personal commitments require clarity sooner, such as a pending job change or a potential geographic move. Strategy is important when choosing the round you'll apply in, but life events don't always align neatly with the admissions calendar.

Finally, remember that round choice isn't just about you; it intersects with your recommenders' bandwidth to get letters written or workload demands that might be put on you if you're currently employed. Applying is not a solo act, so consider the broader ecosystem of people and commitments that affect your readiness.

Build Your List

Applying to business school requires both financial and mental resources. Each application comes with a price tag: fees for the application itself, possible costs for reporting test scores, and in some cases, travel for interviews. You might also work with an MBA admissions consultant who will charge you by the hour or by the school. Multiply all that across several schools, and the costs add up.

 PRO TIP: APPLY FOR FEE WAIVERS

MBA application fees average around $200, with top schools often charging $240 to $275 each, but many programs offer full or partial waivers.[49] You may qualify through financial need, military or service experience, or event attendance. Policies change, so check requirements early and request waivers before paying. These savings add up fast if you're applying to multiple schools.

Time is another cost. Every program you add to your list means drafting or tailoring essays, customizing your résumé, briefing recommenders, and preparing for interviews. You might be surprised by how much effort it takes just to produce one strong application, let alone five or six. The more schools you add, the more you'll need to budget your bandwidth, because a hurried, copy-and-paste application won't stand out. Also, some school applications are longer than others, so be sure to look at the amount and length of essay prompts as you make your decision.

---

49 Marc Ethier, "The MBA App Slump Cost the Top U.S. B-Schools $3,444,990 Last Year," *Poets & Quants*, May 22, 2024, https://poetsandquants.com/2024/05/22/the-mba-app-slump-cost-the-top-u-s-b-schools-3444990-last-year/.

That doesn't mean you should limit yourself to one or two schools if cost and/or time are not a concern. For most applicants, a reasonable approach is to build a portfolio that reflects the following three tiers of ambition:

- **Reach schools** are for when your stats fall below or just at the most recent class profile and when you suspect you might not have a unique enough story to make up for any weaknesses around the metrics. Admission is possible but less predictable.

- **Target schools** are for when your profile aligns closely with the median, giving you a realistic shot if you present a strong case.

- **Safeties** are programs for when your qualifications exceed recent averages, making admission more likely.

This mix gives you options and reduces the risk of being left without an offer while still stretching for the programs that excite you most. And since every application carries a cost in both dollars and energy, being deliberate about how you allocate your efforts will help you approach each one with the focus it deserves.

That said, not everyone approaches the process this way. Some applicants might only apply to the "HSW trinity"—Harvard, Stanford, and Wharton. Or they might apply only to the one or two dream schools, as they define *dream*, and nowhere else. If that is your mindset and those schools are the right fit, there's nothing wrong with having a very short list. But for most candidates, keeping an open mind and building a broader list is the wiser move.

PRO TIP: HOW MANY SCHOOLS SHOULD YOU APPLY TO?

Most MBA applicants submit between five and eight applications, striking a balance between reaching high and playing it safe. Their list typically includes one to three stretch (reach) programs, two to four competitive (target) ones, and one to two safeties, ensuring both ambition and realism.[50]

FIT OVER FOLKLORE

Too often, rankings are the first—and sometimes only—filter applicants use in building their lists. Rankings can be useful, but they're also a distorted lens. Remember that what's considered *elite* depends on your definition of the word. For some applicants, a school in the bottom rungs of the top twenty is the dream; for others, only the M7 will do.

In chapter 4, you explored your goals, values, and the kind of environment where you thrive. Now is the time to apply that self-awareness. Do you prefer a more collaborative or a competitive culture? Do you want to immerse yourself in the energy of an urban campus or settle into the intimacy of a small-town program? Is proximity to an industry hub critical, or would you benefit from stepping away from the noise? One client of mine was determined to go to the best-ranked business school to which she could get accepted. She ended up in a prestigious program that required moving to another region of the country but ended up realizing that the culture wasn't a good match for her. She decided to apply to a lower-ranked school back in her home city, ended up switching to that school, and was much happier being in a location and program that was a better match.

---

50   Linda Abraham, "How Many Schools Should You Apply To?," *Poets & Quants*, May 26, 2017, https://poetsandquants.com/2017/05/26/how-many-schools-should-you-apply-to/.

Once you know your criteria, be deliberate about how you evaluate schools. Match your story with the school's mission statement to evaluate fit. How to do that? Here's one approach: Pick the five to seven factors that matter most to you (e.g., job placement by function or region, teaching style, cohort size, ecosystem of clubs and partners, and alumni engagement), then compare schools against those factors using a simple scoring grid (see figure 5.1). Complement your research with conversations with current students, recent alumni, and (when possible) class visits or virtual sessions to test your assumptions.

MBA 360° Admissions Program Evaluation Mark

Category	Sub-Criteria	Recommended Weight	School A Rating (1-5)	School A Score	School B Rating (1-5)	School B Score	School C Rating (1-5)	School C Score
ROI & Affordability	Tuition, scholarships, salary uplift, debt load	15%	3	0.45				
Brand & Reputation	Prestige, rankings, employer perception	12%	5	0.6				
Career Outcomes	Placement, recruiting access, internships	15%	5	0.75				
Alumni Network	Reach, engagement, mentorship	8%	5	0.4				
Curriculum & Skills	Core, electives, experiential, AI/tech	10%	4	0.4				
Program Format & Structure	FT/PT/online fit, length, flexibility	7%	3	0.21				
Location & Mobility	Cost of living, industry proximity, visas	10%	3	0.3				
Culture & Peer Group	Diversity, vibe, collaboration	7%	4	0.28				
Faculty & Resources	Teaching quality, research centers, services	6%	4	0.24				
Values & Mission Alignment	DEI, sustainability, ethics	5%	3	0.15				
Personal/Family Considerations	Partner career, housing, childcare, lifestyle	5%	5	0.25				
	SCHOOL SCORE:	100%		4.03				

Along the way, watch for patterns or red flags rather than putting too much stock in isolated anecdotes or biased sources. Keep in mind that many schools describe themselves in similar ways, such as having a collaborative culture. Trust your instincts about what feels real and right for you.

Once you've built your list, step back and take a holistic look. Does it balance ambition and pragmatism? Does it cover your likely post-MBA career moves? Have you accounted for personal life, family (as relevant), location, and cost? And most importantly: Does at least one program feel like a true fit, regardless of prestige?

Test Scores and Transcripts

Submitting your GMAT, GRE, or other standardized test scores and ensuring your transcripts arrive on time may not be the most thrilling part of the admissions journey, but it is essential. Missing or delayed submissions can stall your application in the review queue. Build a checklist of each school's requirements and track completion carefully. Note that some schools will accept unofficial score reports but then require official reports should you be accepted to the program.

Test results serve as a proof point of academic readiness, especially quantitative skills, and many schools will accept the highest score if you retake an exam. So don't hesitate to try again if you believe you can improve. If a school offers a test waiver, you'll still need to demonstrate academic ability elsewhere through a strong GPA, quantitative coursework successfully completed, or analytical work experience. A waiver doesn't mean you are off the hook!

Most schools require official transcripts from every institution where you have earned credits. Order these early, especially if you studied abroad or attended multiple universities, as processing can take weeks. If your GPA is on the lower side, a higher test score can help offset that concern. Conversely, if your test score is weaker, strong academic transcripts or professional achievements can provide reassurance. Plenty of students are admitted below the published median, while others with perfect scores are turned away. Numbers matter, but they never tell the whole story of what you bring to the table. For what it's worth, I've had more prospective students seeking advice on applying with a low GPA. If this is you, first, realize that you are not alone. Second, focus on providing additional proof points, such as a specialized master's program in a quantitative subject before applying to an MBA. Yes, it could push you into a future cycle, but you will be applying from a position of greater strength.

Recommendations: Third-Party Proof

Your recommendations provide third-party proof of what you claim in your résumé and essays. Admissions officers want to know: How do others experience you? What do your colleagues and supervisors say about the way you lead, contribute, and grow? Many recommendations focus on how you compare to your peers and how you respond to constructive feedback.

In recent years, business schools have responded to the concern about the burden on recommenders when an applicant is applying to multiple schools. As a result, many schools use the common letter of recommendation, so your recommender only has to submit one recommendation.

CHOOSE INSIGHT OVER PRESTIGE

Many applicants are tempted to try to gain an edge by having a recommendation from a prominent person. A lukewarm letter from a high-ranking executive, however, is far less effective than a detailed letter from someone who knows you well and has actually worked with you day to day. Admissions officers read thousands of recommendations and can tell the difference between a generic endorsement and a letter that comes to life with stories. Choose recommenders who know you well and can speak to how you influenced a consequential project's direction, the measurable outcome of your work, how you've responded when faced with setbacks, or other concrete examples.

And don't be afraid to think outside the box. One applicant was a volunteer for a major women's civic and community leadership organization and chose to have her committee chair write her second recommendation. This was a smart strategy because the choice aligned perfectly with a business school that values community engagement. The recommender addressed how the applicant led fundraising initiatives and collaborated in teams to make decisions. The letter provided convincing evidence of her fit for that particular business school, and she was accepted.

Admissions officers know when a letter is genuine. One authentic voice, backed by specifics, will always carry more weight than generic platitudes.

 ## PRO TIP: DON'T LOOK AT ALUMNI AS YOUR TICKET IN

If you think you are standing out by asking for a letter of recommendation from an alum, I'm sorry to have to point this out to you: You're not the only one doing that! Don't hesitate to seek a recommendation from an alum if that person knows you well and can speak to your qualities and experiences as relevant for an MBA and for the particular school. But just know that having the endorsement of an alum won't necessarily be a differentiating factor.

SET THEM UP FOR SUCCESS

While you shouldn't script their letters, you can set your recommenders up for success by briefing them on the why and what of your application strategy. Provide context about why you're applying now and what you hope to do with your MBA. Remind them of projects you worked on together and outcomes you achieved. That way, they can frame their stories in a way that complements the themes you're emphasizing in your own materials.

Also help them understand the culture and curriculum of the school. Share the mission statement with them. They will write a stronger recommendation about your fit if they understand more about the program. Make it easy for them logistically with reminders and timelines so they can write a strong letter in a timely fashion with minimal stress. Some schools, such as Duke Fuqua, give a week's grace period to recommenders.

The importance of consistency comes up again here. Your recommendations don't stand alone; they should reinforce the larger narrative, bring to life the experiences you might have talked about in your essays, and provide evidence of the claims you make in your résumé. Recommendations echo your story but also add fresh perspective, showing the admissions readers a side of you that you can't present yourself.

Strategic Résumés

Think of your résumé as the movie trailer for your candidacy. It isn't meant to be a complete catalog; it's a highlight reel that gives the admissions committee a clear sense of your scope and impact. Admissions officers scan for evidence of leadership, results, growth, and potential.

A strategic résumé does the following three things:

1. **Shows impact.** Use numbers, percentages, and metrics to make outcomes, such as revenues increased, costs reduced, or partnerships expanded, tangible. Even if your role doesn't lend itself easily to quantification, think about the reach of the projects you've delivered, the innovative approaches you've initiated, the skills you've demonstrated to carry out the work, or other examples of impact, influence, and growth.

2. **Signals leadership.** Admissions officers want to see you as someone who others follow, not just someone who executes tasks. That doesn't mean you need a formal management title. It could mean spearheading a cross-functional initiative, mentoring junior colleagues, or being tapped to represent your team in front of senior leadership.

3. **Demonstrates growth.** The best résumés tell a story of momentum. Each role shows progression, whether in responsibility, influence, or complexity. Even lateral moves can signal growth if you frame them as broadening your experience or building a new skill set.

 ## PRO TIP: EVERYTHING MUST HAVE A PURPOSE

For every bullet point in the work experience section of your résumé, ask yourself, So what? How does this contribute to telling my overall story? Why should they care?

LESS IS MORE

Don't fall into the trap of cluttering your résumé with too much detail. Applicants sometimes provide long lists of routine duties or include just about everything they've ever done academically, professionally, and in extracurriculars in the hope that more is better. It isn't. Admissions officers have limited time and are looking for clarity. They are also reading many files, not just yours. Make it easy for them to make sense of who you are and what you have done. Give them a concise, one-page document (aim for a page for every ten years of experience) that makes your trajectory obvious and your impact undeniable.

THE MYTH OF THE SMALL STUFF

Applicants often tie themselves in knots over minor details—a comma out of place, a missing period at the end of a bullet, or in their résumés. These are worth attending to, of course. Proofreading, good grammar, and overall polish signal care and professionalism. However, a résumé that demonstrates measurable outcomes and progression will always carry more weight than one that is technically perfect but uninspired. Small errors may be noticed, but they don't outweigh the larger narrative.

In chapter 6 we're going to talk about how we humans often gravitate toward controllable tasks, such as proofreading, when outcomes feel uncertain. Fixating on minutiae can provide temporary comfort but doesn't move the needle. Your energy is better spent making your résumé clear and persuasive. So, by all means, proofread carefully and ask someone else to review your materials. Just don't let the pursuit of flawlessness eclipse the real task, which is using your résumé to provide a persuasive argument of why you deserve a seat.

PRO TIP: LEAD WITH THE LEDE

Anchor attention on your résumé where it matters most by leading with your most compelling bullet in each role. The serial-position effect, supported by cognitive research, shows that early items in a list are more likely to be remembered and perceived as important, thanks to the primacy effect.[51] That opening bullet earns prime real estate.

Finally, remember that your résumé doesn't stand alone. It works in tandem with your essays and recommendations, reinforcing the same themes. Where essays may show the why behind your choices, your résumé shows the impact of your choices. Done well, it helps the committee see you as a candidate with not only a record of accomplishment but also the potential to contribute meaningfully to their class.

Essays: Show Them Who You Are

Your application as a whole is an exercise in persuasion, but the essay portion is especially so. The purpose of an essay is not to showcase all of your achievements, the breadth of your vocabulary, or your ability to sound impressive but to make it easy for the admissions committee to understand who you are, what drives you, and what you will bring to their program. This connects to the work you did in chapter 4. There, you clarified the themes that run through your life and career—your motivations, values, and experiences that have shaped you—and identified your strengths and value proposition. Those themes are your raw material that you now put to work in your essays.

---

51   Alex Birkett, "The Serial Position Effect: Why Primacy and Order Matter in Psychology," *CXL*, December 25, 2022, https://cxl.com/blog/serial-position-effect/.

Essay prompts run the gamut from straightforward, such as LBS asking you to describe your post-MBA goals and how their program will contribute toward those, to Duke Fuqua's "25 Random Things About Me"! Prompts can get quite creative: HEC Paris has asked applicants to imagine and describe leading a life totally different from the one they have now.

 ## PRO TIP: WRITE CLEARLY

Your essays should be well written, but they are not entries in a creative writing contest (even if the prompt itself is creative). Instead, they are a tool for strategy and persuasion. Strong essays bring the reader into your story, and in doing so, they persuade the reader that you deserve one of the coveted seats in the program.

ANSWER THE QUESTION!

This advice may sound obvious, but the most important thing you can do to make your essay effective is to answer the prompt. It's also easy advice to follow: Simply answer the question being asked or reply to the prompt provided and do so within the word count range requested. This is another example of "It's not all about you." Schools aren't providing space for you just to show off your achievements; rather, they want to understand how you show up, how you think, and how you thrive, in various environments and situations. If they're asking you to write about a time when you worked on a team and faced a challenge, but instead, you decide to tell them about a major solo achievement, you've missed the mark. Even if that solo story feels more impressive to you, it doesn't answer the question. You're doing yourself a disservice by substituting *Y* when they asked for *X*.

The same holds true for multipart questions. Look at one of the Michigan Ross MBA essay prompts for the 2025–2026 cycle: "What is your short-term career goal, and how will Ross' philosophy in Action-Based Learning help you achieve it? Please be specific. Please answer both parts of this question. (300 words)." Answering both parts of the question might seem like easy instructions to follow, but you might get so caught up in responding to one part that you neglect the other. They probably wouldn't put the reminder in if they hadn't seen essays make that mistake before!

And then there are prompts that are on the long side, with higher word counts for your response. Be sure to read those carefully so that you don't gloss over important details. Take this Kellogg prompt as an example: "Intentionality is a key aspect of what makes our graduates successful Kellogg leaders. Help us understand your journey by articulating your motivations for pursuing an MBA, the specific goals you aim to achieve, and why you believe now is the right moment. Moreover, share why you feel Kellogg is best suited to serve as a catalyst for your career aspirations and what you will contribute to our community of lifelong learners during your time here. (450 words)."

My advice for these lengthier essays is not to panic but to dissect the prompt (like you might have done in elementary school to learn grammar and sentence structure). For example, to tackle the Kellog prompt, break it down into manageable chunks and complete these sentences from the prompt:

My motivations for pursuing an MBA are …
The specific goals I aim to achieve are …
Now is the right moment for an MBA because …

Then think about how you would answer the following:

Why do I feel that Kellogg is best suited for my career aspirations? How will I contribute to the community?

Once you get the core elements nailed down, see how they all hang together. Smooth out the flow and polish the wording so it reflects the caliber of an essay for graduate school.

MAKE EVERY WORD COUNT

Some essays are short, such as UCLA Anderson's request that you answer in 150 words, "Why is the MBA the right degree for you to pursue both personally and professionally?" while others can be much longer, such as requiring a *minimum* 250-word response to "How will the Booth MBA help you achieve your immediate and long-term post-MBA career goals?"

Many applicants struggle to say everything they want to say in a short space, but this is an exercise in focusing on what is truly most important, what will move the needle in a strategic way. You must market yourself concisely.

Substance should outweigh padding. Just as with résumés, a common misstep in essays is trying to include every project, client, or life experience for fear of leaving anything out. That approach usually backfires. A scattered or cluttered essay is hard to follow and forgettable. Instead, select an example that directly relates to the prompt and develop it fully. For example, if you're applying to INSEAD and see their prompt, "Describe a highly stressful situation you faced and how you managed it. What did this experience teach you about yourself and your interactions with others? (400 words maximum)," show not just what you did but also how you thought, how you influenced others, and how the experience shaped your growth.

A reliable way to keep focus is to give each essay a single "job." Essay prompts might ask you to demonstrate leadership, global perspective, social impact, resilience, or career vision. Focus on that one theme and go deep. An essay that accomplishes its single purpose will do far more for you than one that throws out everything at once to impress the reader, especially when they didn't ask for everything.

VARIATIONS ON A THEME

Many schools have introduced variety to the essay portion of their applications in recent years. These variations include the following:

Video Essays

INSEAD and Georgetown McDonough are two examples of business schools that require a video essay in addition to written ones. The purpose is to see how you communicate spontaneously and authentically, like you would in class, without the benefit of endless drafting and revision. You'll typically have two chances to record your response, so if your first attempt doesn't go well, you can scrap it and try one more time.

You may or may not know the question in advance, but you can find some prior prompts online. For instance, in the 2025–2026 cycle, a Berkeley Haas video essay prompt was, "Briefly introduce yourself to the admissions committee, explain which Defining Leadership Principle resonates most with you, and tell us how you have exemplified the principle in your personal or professional life. Please review the Defining Leadership Principles in advance and take time to prepare your answer before recording. You will be able to test your audio-visual connection before recording. Video essays should last 1-2 minutes and may not exceed 2 minutes."

And Georgetown has used this one: "We believe a vibrant community is built on diverse and unique individuals, and we want you to bring your whole self to Georgetown McDonough. We've learned about your professional and leadership qualities throughout the application, but now we want to know more about you beyond work. Whether it's a new hobby, a fun adventure, or a simple pleasure, *in one minute*, share what has recently brought you joy outside of work."[52]

Whatever the prompt is, don't worry that you need to hire Steven Spielberg to direct your response video. You aren't competing for best cinematography in the academy awards—you're authentically showing who you are!

Picture Essays

Photo essays are a creative spin on traditional written essays, inviting candidates to reflect on the significance of one or more images. Instead of responding to a written prompt, you choose one photo. Chicago Booth's recent prompt presented four photos symbolizing the program's core values and asked applicants to choose one and explain how the image resonates with their own values.

NYU Stern takes this idea a step further with its "Pick Six" essay, asking applicants to select and submit six images of their own choosing—photos, drawings, or other visuals—that capture their interests, values, or personality. Each image is to be accompanied by a brief caption and a short overview, allowing candidates to showcase their individuality and creativity in a format that goes beyond traditional written essays.[53]

---

52 "Georgetown McDonough MBA Essay Analysis 2025–2026," Clear Admit, https://www.clearadmit.com/mba-admissions-essay-topics-analyses/ mcdonough-mba-essay-topic-analysis/.

53 "Stern MBA Essays & Analysis 2025–2026," Clear Admit, https://www.clearadmit. com/mba-admissions-essay-topics-analyses/nyu-stern-essay-topic-analysis/.

Rice Business gives you the choice of providing your own photo or just describing it: "While we know a picture is worth 1,000 words, in 500 words or less tell us the story of a photo of your choosing that has significant value in your life experiences. Please feel free to share your photo!

You can complete this essay via a traditional written response (500-word limit) or via a video response (one to three-minute time limit)."

These essays encourage authenticity and reflection. Don't just describe what the image shows; share why it speaks to you and how it connects to your lived experiences. Writing concisely and purposefully is key. For example, if responding to the Booth prompt, focus on one or two meaningful anecdotes that the photo calls to mind, clearly tie your values to Booth's, and convey how you'll contribute to their collaborative, curious community.

 PRO TIP: DON'T OVERFOCUS ON FORMAT

It is easy to fall into the trap of worrying needlessly about the hidden agenda of different essay formats, such as which photo is the best one to choose to answer the Chicago Booth essay prompt. The fact of the matter is that admissions officers have to read a lot of applications, so varying essay topics and formats helps them get to know applicants from various angles, not to mention that it keeps their job from becoming monotonous as they read many essays for the same prompt each admissions cycle. It's serious, hard work to select talent from a large application pool, so part of your job is to make it easier for them. Once again, we see that "it's not just about you"!

Optional Essays

Some schools provide additional prompts that are optional. These give you the chance to explain aspects of your background that add value but don't fit elsewhere, such as a period when you stepped out of the workforce to care for an aging parent or deal with an illness or a long gap in employment after a layoff.

Framed thoughtfully, these stories don't just explain gaps or other idiosyncrasies in your application; they demonstrate empathy, perspective, and resilience—qualities that enrich a business school cohort. Just make sure you use them wisely. They aren't an overflow space for additional content you wanted to share in the primary essay.

KEEP IT REAL

A common mistake applicants make is overengineering their essays. When you include superfluous phrasing or stack the page with fancy words you'd never use in regular conversation, you risk obscuring your point. I'm reminded of an undergrad classmate of mine who wanted to sound more sophisticated in an essay and described his burger and fries at McDonald's as a "repast."

Also, get to the point quickly. If the question asks about a time you faced an ethical dilemma, start by naming the dilemma and the stakes involved, then describe the decisions you made, the impact, and what you learned.

Adding concise, colorful details can help the reader visualize the story; a quick description of where you were when this happened or what season of the year it was can make the experience come alive. You want to bring the reader into your world as if they are walking alongside you, directly experiencing what you are sharing. Varying the length of sentences in your essay can create rhythm that draws readers in and keeps them engaged.

PRO TIP: CLEAN, SIMPLE STRUCTURE

Make your writing easy to follow from a macro level (well-organized thoughts that flow in a logical way) to the micro (clean sentence structure, correct grammar, punctuation that does its job). If the admissions officer has to stop and reread a sentence to figure out what you mean or has to go back to a prior paragraph to try to follow the story, you've lost them. Clean, simple writing is also more persuasive because it creates positive feelings and makes readers more receptive to the message. In short, pay attention to the cognitive ease of your essays; don't make extra work for the readers to try to stay engaged or to figure out what you are saying.

DON'T WRITE FROM THE SCHOOL WEBSITE

When a school asks why you want to join their program, don't fall into the trap of simply repeating what's on their website. Generic statements about "world-class faculty" or "global alumni networks" are not persuasive. Instead, connect the dots between your goals and what the school specifically offers: a lab where you'll test your ideas, a recruiting pipeline into your chosen industry, a learning method that matches your style. You do want to study their website so that you can connect your story to their value proposition to show true fit, but you should tell the story of that connection in your own specific words.

PRO TIP: COMMON PITFALLS
TO AVOID IN ESSAYS

- **Trying to reuse an essay.** Make sure you're addressing the prompt at hand and tailoring your response to the school's culture, not recycling an essay you wrote for another school's prompt.

- **Overexplaining the setup.** Keep context brief. Use your word count for the decision, the action, and the outcome.

- **Describing generic ambition.** "I want to make an impact" is vague. Spell out where, how, and why.

- **Showing performative vulnerability.** Don't dramatize setbacks just for effect. Show how you exercised judgment and grew.

- **Rehashing your résumé.** Essays should add perspective and depth, not repeat bullet points from your résumé.

- **Not balancing who you are with what you've done.** While the balance depends on the prompt, you usually want to talk not just about your experiences and achievements but about what those reveal about your character and strengths.

- **Falling into the "here's what I've achieved" temptation.** As the saying goes, there is no "I" in team. It's not all about *you*! Where relevant, depending on the prompt, bring in team efforts, not just individual ones, and showcase times you've done things in service to others or a joint mission.

- ***Being superficial instead of vulnerable.*** Don't shy away from recounting failures or challenging experiences. The MBA is about growth, and they want to see how you have responded to growth opportunities. If you were perfect, why would you need the MBA?

- **Overengineering.** Avoid fussing with words for polish's sake. Clear, persuasive content beats pretentious wording every time. Write to explain, not to impress.
- **Obsessing over proofreading.** As with your résumé, clean copy matters, but one typo won't sink you. Focus your energy on clarity and persuasion—the parts that actually move the needle. I would be surprised if eleven-time Olympic medalist Simone Biles did not get an interview at HBS because she missed a single comma in her essay.

Interviews: The Final Gatekeeper

If you've been invited to an interview, congratulations! You've cleared a significant hurdle. The interview stage signals that the admissions committee considers you a viable candidate.

WHY INTERVIEWS MATTER

Think of the interview as a chance to humanize your candidacy. Admissions readers have an initial impression of you from your application materials. Interviews then give them the opportunity to reality-check that impression, to see how you will show up on campus. Interviews are also a way for schools to assess who you are beyond the credentials and qualities described in your application. Admissions interviewers want to know what you're like (or who you are or how you show up) in person. Again, this goes back to the concept of authenticity that business schools are assessing in the selection process.

In addition, they want to avoid admitting any bad apples. My clients often find that my analogy of going through TSA at the airport illustrates this point well. TSA officers want to make sure you don't have any hazardous materials on you before you board the plane, while admissions officers need to make sure you don't have any "onboard luggage" that would be a detriment in the classroom. So, whether it's lithium-ion batteries or a ruthless personality, gate-keepers at airports and in admissions offices want to make sure you don't set off any alarms!

PREPARING STRATEGICALLY

Be ready to articulate your story in a way that connects the dots of your past experience, your MBA goals, and why their program is a good match. Also be crystal clear on the key messages you want to convey.

Key strategic points include the following:

- You won't be able to anticipate every question, but be prepared to answer the questions, Why an MBA? Why this school? Why now? And why are you a fit?

- Familiarize yourself with prior interview questions to get a feel for what might come up. Look up reports online through Clear Admit and GMAT Club that post questions asked to previous candidates to get a feel for what you might be asked.

- Practice giving concise answers for open-ended questions, such as "Walk me through your résumé."

- Anticipate the obvious behavior-based questions (e.g., Tell me about a time when you ...). Practice by using the STAR method (describe the situation or task, the actions you took, and the results or outcomes achieved). Don't memorize stock answers or try to guess the right thing to say. Schools can see through rehearsed responses.

- Be ready to bring your résumé to life, not just to recite what they've already read.

- Have one or two talking points in your back pocket that you can weave into the conversation when and if the opportunity is presented. These can be fun facts about yourself and your life—the sorts of things that add interest to your overall presentation of who you are and aren't likely to be on your résumé.

- Research the people who might be interviewing you and their roles. Look them up on LinkedIn to see what they post about and what values they highlight. You might share a common interest or gain other small insights that will help you connect authentically.

- Keep in mind that different interviewers—staff, faculty, alumni—will bring different motivations and perspectives to the conversation. When I worked in admissions, for example, the program director and I had very different approaches in how we conducted interviews, based on what was important to us. Two candidates could interview for the same program but have completely different interview experiences. And the challenge is that you don't always know which person you will meet with. So, do research the interviewers, as suggested above, but don't assume you can know how they're going to approach the interview.

- Watch YouTube videos of admissions staff speaking at information sessions to get a sense of their cadence and style. Read about the benefits of linguistic mirroring for some tips on being more persuasive through nonverbal communication.[54]

- Some schools—MIT Sloan, for example—ask you to respond to two short-answer questions no later than twenty-four hours before your interview.[55] Be prepared to elaborate on your essay response when you get into the interview, if the same topic comes up. (Some schools, such as HBS, even have a post-interview reflection, so the interview itself can come with pre- and post-hoops to jump through!)

PRO TIP: BUILD A "SKILLS MIRROR"

When you frame your strengths during the application process, mirror the five soft skills employers say they want *after* you graduate, and back each one with an example of how you've demonstrated that skill. Think: problem-solving, communication, strategic thinking, interpersonal/teamwork, and adaptability.[56] Draft a two- to three-sentence story for each, and echo those same five skills across your résumé bullets, essays, and interview answers so the through line is unmistakable.

---

54   Brian Lufkin, "How 'Linguistic Mirroring' Can Make You More Con-
      vincing," *BBC*, December 21, 2020, https://www.bbc.com/worklife/
      article/20201214-how-linguistic-mirroring-can-make-you-more-convincing.

55   "Preparing for Your Interview," MIT Sloan School of Management,
      accessed November 19, 2025, https://mitsloan.mit.edu/admissions/
      preparing-for-your-interview.

56   Daisy Culleton, "MBA Resume: 5 Skills Employers Want from Business School
      Grads," *BusinessBecause*, May 12, 2025, https://www.businessbecause.com/news/
      mba-jobs/7213/mba-resume-skills-employers-want.

DURING THE INTERVIEW

Applicants often assume the interview is solely about them in the spotlight. In reality, interviewers are evaluating how you'll align with the institution's culture, needs, and values. Sometimes those needs aren't visible to you, such as filling an industry gap in recruiting or ensuring geographic diversity.

Most interviews are one-on-one, but some schools add extra evaluative elements such as video responses or group exercises. In team-based exercises, schools are less interested in the smartest insight and more in how you engage. Do you notice quiet voices and draw them in, or do you dominate the room? Even small, unexpected moments can reveal more than rehearsed answers: One candidate impressed the admissions committee by staying calm when her cat jumped onto the keyboard during a video interview! One of my clients, a CPA, subtly shifted stereotypical perceptions of accountants at my suggestion by adding a family photo in the background of his video, softening a numbers-only image.

 ## PRO TIP: LEARN FROM THE TED KENNEDY MOMENT

While applying to an MBA program isn't exactly like running for office, there are similarities because they are both campaigns of persuasion. Your job is to get the admissions committee to vote for you. With that said, don't make the mistake of not being able to answer *why* you're doing what you're doing. In a televised interview with CBS during the campaign for the 1980 presidential election, Senator Ted Kennedy famously hesitated and rambled when asked, "Why do you want to be president?"

This was such a fundamental question, yet he couldn't answer clearly. Decades later, it is still remembered as a campaign-breaker. Never let that happen to you—practice clear, confident responses to foundational questions about why you want an MBA, why from that school, and why now.[57]

Your Bottom Line

The MBA application process is complex, but it is also within your control—at least the parts that matter most. Like the impactful business leader you are, or aim to become, you must gather input, weigh perspectives, and make tough calls, but ultimately, the decisions are yours.

Across all elements of your application, present a coherent and authentic story that aligns with your goals from chapter 4 and that shows the admissions committee why you would be a great addition to their next class.

Remember that what carries the most weight is your ability to help the admissions committee make an informed decision by offering a candidacy that is clear, consistent, and compelling. Of course, there are some givens—deadlines have to be met, test scores reported, transcripts ordered, and recommenders encouraged to follow through on time, but that's only the bare minimum. And, sure, numbers from GPAs and test scores are important, but they aren't the whole story. If you can tell a compelling story, you will not only survive this demanding application process but will gain a lifelong superpower to advocate for yourself and your future.

---

57   Kaleena Fraga, "'The Question': Ted Kennedy & the Pitfalls of Running for President, History First, February 4, 2019, https://history-first.com/2019/02/04/the-question-ted-kennedy-the-pitfalls-of-running-for-president/.

Speaking of decisions, chapter 7, The Power Shift, talks about what happens after you click "submit," when you'll find the balance of power tilting as you wait for an answer and after you get the answer. But first, in chapter 6, let's look at the psychology of applications—how to manage the emotions that can come as you move through the application process.

YOUR STRATEGIC SWOT

- Am I applying in the round that best matches both my readiness and my goals?

- Does my school list balance reach, target, and safety options in a way that fits my priorities and maximizes my chances of acceptance?

- Do my essays, résumé, and recommendations consistently reinforce the same themes?

- Have I addressed any concerns about GPA or test scores with offsets or context?

- Have I chosen recommenders who know me well and can offer credible examples?

CHAPTER 6

The Psychology of Applications

Applying to business school can feel like being on an emotional roller coaster. You might find yourself riding the highs and lows, from confidence and optimism to self-doubt and second-guessing. These are not signs of weakness. They are normal reactions when pursuing something as important to your professional advancement as an MBA and when you consider how much of the process can feel out of your control.

Maybe you're one of the lucky ones who sails right through the process with minimal distress or angst. You position yourself strategically, as discussed in chapter 4, and you work diligently through the application steps, as covered in chapter 5. If so, congratulations! But if you're like most applicants, you'll find yourself hopping on that roller coaster somewhere along the way. You might feel overwhelmed, stuck, pessimistic, or just generally uncomfortable at some point. That's why I consider this chapter on the psychology of applying to be one of the most important ones in the book.

I can't be your therapist, but I can share what has worked for my clients as they deal with the emotional side of MBA applications.

We'll take a look at typical challenges applicants face at each stage of the journey, and I'll offer practical strategies for managing the emotional fallout.

Craving Certainty

Sometimes I get asked what the percentage likelihood is that someone will be admitted to their dream MBA program. The honest answer is I don't know. Sure, I can take a look at your entire profile: test scores, undergraduate GPA, recommendations, the cohesion and uniqueness of your story, and how well you fit with the priority criteria and culture of a particular program. I can help you understand where your strengths lie or where the competition might have an edge. That informed perspective allows me to offer a realistic sense of your positioning. Ultimately, though, the answer is, "It depends."

Once again, our "It's not about you" premise comes into play. If getting in were only about how your GPA, test scores, and professional background stack up against static measures admissions teams use, then we could do much better than educated predictions. But acceptance criteria are a moving target, as each school assembles a cohort that takes into consideration the application pool for that particular year. As a result, you can meet or surpass every threshold for the quantitative metrics and have a distinctive story to tell yet still not be accepted. That can obviously be frustrating for you, but admissions offices find it really difficult, too. Every selective school will tell you that they often have to reject amazing candidates in favor of equally amazing candidates who just happen to be a better fit for a given year's class and strategic direction as established by school leadership.

It makes complete sense that the question "Can you give me a percentage?" comes up when I speak with prospective applicants.

When stakes are high and outcomes are uncertain, the need for clarity intensifies. We humans crave answers because uncertainty feels way too uncomfortable. Psychologists call this craving a need for cognitive closure, which refers to our desire for definitive answers and resolution when faced with uncertainty. Achieving cognitive closure can soothe the discomfort of not knowing, even if the conclusions we settle on are inaccurate.[58]

For example, I could answer that request for a percentage by saying there's only a 15 percent chance the applicant will get into Columbia. While such a low percentage is not, objectively, good news, having any answer at all may be received emotionally as good news. Any percentage is better than no percentage! And there you have the danger of our natural tendency to want to pluck certainty out of uncertainty: This drive can narrow our thinking and prompt us to cling to premature, unfounded, or incorrect answers and to resist new or nuanced information.

HOW TO COPE WITH UNCERTAINTY

Uncertainty is a constant throughout the MBA admissions journey, from the earliest stages of researching programs and gauging your chances to waiting for interview invitations and final decisions. While it's tempting to chase definitive answers at every turn, a more effective approach is to focus on navigating each stage with composure and clarity. Coping well with uncertainty means building habits and perspectives that help you stay steady even when the next step isn't clear. Here are some practical ways to do that.

---

58   Jessica Koehler, "Navigating the Paradox of Certainty and Uncertainty," *Psychology Today*, October 11, 2024, https://www.psychologytoday.com/us/blog/beyond-school-walls/202410/navigating-the-paradox-of-certainty-and-uncertainty.

Mindfulness and Present Focus

Practicing mindfulness helps reduce future-focused anxiety. Staying grounded in the present through breathing, journaling, or meditation can quiet the mental spiral and build steadiness amid unpredictability.

Acceptance and Distress Tolerance

Acknowledge the urge for a definitive answer, then gently let it go. Over time, the act of sitting with uncertainty without reacting helps you feel more at ease and can quiet the emotional turbulence that comes with nervous anticipation.

Prepare for Multiple Outcomes

Mentally exploring different scenarios helps moderate emotional responses. If things don't go as you hoped, you'll be better prepared; if they do, you'll appreciate the good news all the more.

Find Anchors

Create stability by leaning on predictable routines, finding moments of gratitude, and making space for humor and self-compassion. Structure, small joys, and emotional self-kindness can stabilize you when external outcomes feel up in the air. I've had clients focus on self-care and consistent routines as outlets for their stress, such as the applicant who upped his sessions at the gym to ninety minutes instead of his usual forty-five. Others find ways to treat themselves with rewards along the way, such as my client from Europe who bought herself jewelry each time she completed a step in the admissions journey to an M7 school. Your reward doesn't have to be something that sparkles, but small treats for yourself at key milestones can be predictable, comforting anchors.

Becoming more comfortable with uncertainty is a valuable skill at every point in the application process. These strategies help you stay balanced and engaged, setting you up for the next step: recognizing where you do have influence and letting go of what you can't control.

 PRO TIP: PREP FOR STRESS LIKE YOU PREP FOR TESTS

No matter which techniques you use to cope with the emotional ups and downs of the MBA application process, be sure to prepare for the stress before it hits. You don't want to be blindsided and scrambling for coping strategies at the peak of pressure. Put measures in place as soon as possible, ideally before deadlines loom. I call this stress prep. Just as you might take a test prep course to prepare for the GMAT, engage in your own stress prep. Give yourself the advantage of being ready with routines, support, and strategies so that when the anxiety spikes, you can stay steady.

Control What You Can, Let Go of the Rest

Control and certainty are intertwined, but they're not the same: Certainty is about knowing, while control is about doing. When we can't be sure of an outcome, we often pour energy into tasks we can do, even if they don't matter much.

Our craving for certainty often drives us to overcontrol. We cling to small, manageable details in hopes of securing outcomes we actually can't guarantee. In MBA applications, that could mean attending every information session when one or two would do, obsessing over the placement of a comma in an essay, or searching the web for every possible interview question that has been asked and memorizing it, as if mastering minutiae would somehow shield us from uncertainty.

These behaviors reflect two well-established and heavily researched psychological concepts: locus of control and illusion of control. Locus of control refers to the degree to which people believe they can influence life events. A strong internal orientation (internal locus of control) can inspire confidence and drive, but it also tempts us to overmanage areas that don't matter that much.[59] Similarly, the illusion of control describes our tendency to overestimate our influence over outcomes, especially when we're deeply invested in success.[60] Both concepts help explain why applicants often double down on low-impact actions, mistakenly equating busyness with effectiveness.

Remember those cautions in chapter 5 about not overly sweating the small stuff? Obsessing over details that don't move the needle, such as deciding whether to use Times New Roman or Arial for the essay font, feels comforting because those details are controllable. Fixating on them provides a temporary sense of stability in a process that feels unpredictable, but it doesn't lead to better outcomes.

As an applicant, you have the most control early in the process: choosing programs wisely, timing applications strategically, crafting a clear story, and selecting strong recommenders. Once you hit "submit," control largely shifts to the admissions committees that weigh factors

---

59　Ágnes Szabó-Morvai and Hubert János Kiss, "Locus of Control, Educational Attainment, and College Aspirations: The Relative Role of Effort and Expectations," *Education Economics* 32, no. 6 (2023): 862–81, https://www.tandfonline.com/doi/full/10.1080/09645292.2023.2273220.

60　Bryce Hoffman, "Think You're in Control? The Surprising Ways Illusions of Control Fool Us," *Forbes*, September 29, 2024, https://www.forbes.com/sites/brycehoffman/2024/09/29/think-youre-in-control-the-surprising-ways-illusions-of-control-fool-us/.

beyond your reach as we've talked about in prior chapters. Trying to micromanage every detail won't change this dynamic; you're only draining your energy that could be better spent on high-impact efforts.

HOW TO RESIST THE URGE TO OVERCONTROL

Some of the strategies for coping with uncertainty offered earlier also apply here, but these additional practices can help you resist the urge to overcontrol more effectively.

Clarify What Truly Matters

Identify the application elements that genuinely influence outcomes, such as your narrative coherence, leadership examples, and fit with the program, and focus your energy on those.

Set Boundaries on Perfectionism

Perfectionism can quietly sabotage progress. It may feel like you're striving for excellence, but research, and countless examples I've observed among my clients, shows how perfectionism leads to exhaustion and stagnation.[61] Setting realistic standards and allowing room for what truly matters keeps you moving forward.

Use the Impact Test

Before obsessing over a revision or detail, pause and ask, Is this change helpful for the reader? Is this likely to influence an admissions decision? If not, it's probably not worth the time.

---

61   Leslie Jamison, "The Pain of Perfectionism," *The New Yorker*, August 4, 2025, https://www.newyorker.com/magazine/2025/08/11/the-pain-of-perfectionism.

Invite Feedback

Instead of repeatedly polishing the same section, get input from mentors, peers, or professional reviewers. Fresh perspectives help you exit revision loops and refocus on substance. ChatGPT or Grok, used responsibly, can also be your friend.

Practice Letting Go

When the urge to overcontrol arises, pause, label it, and gently redirect your focus to actions that align with your priorities.

Learning to resist the pull of overcontrol frees up mental bandwidth for the parts of the process you *can* influence. Paired with your growing ability to tolerate uncertainty, this skill will not only strengthen your application experience but will also prepare you for future leadership challenges where discernment, not micromanagement, can set you apart.

PRO TIP: DIG YOURSELF OUT OF INFORMATION OVERLOAD

The internet makes it easy to drown in MBA admissions content—websites, rankings, forums, and endless social media feeds. Seeking more information feels like a way to minimize uncertainty and gain control, but overconsumption often raises more questions than it answers and can fuel anxiety.

Moreover, you will often find conflicting advice on the internet or even in real life. I once had a question about a client and asked a couple of my peers for their thoughts. Two industry veterans gave me completely different answers. This is normal, as we each bring our own perspectives, opinions, and experiences to any question. I knew how to parse the conflicting answers, but if you don't work in this space, it's harder to make sense of conflicting information. So, when in doubt, get information directly from the school when possible, and in other cases, trust your own critical thinking. If you are applying to business school, you already have a good head on your shoulders!

Also, instead of chasing every detail, focus on meaningful signals and tune out the noise. One key insight you pick up by attending a school's information webinar is worth more than many hours spent dissecting message boards. Information should serve your strategy, not become a substitute for it.

When Your Confidence Is Shaken

Even the most accomplished applicants can find their confidence rattled during the MBA admissions process. Business school websites and blogs are designed to showcase the school's value proposition in the most impressive way and can therefore intimidate even the most confident applicant. Schools highlight successful alumni, rankings stories fuel elitism, and online chatter often treats programs as though they exist on a single, unquestionable hierarchy. Add to this the flood of social media posts and applicant forums, and it's easy to feel like you don't measure up.

This self-doubt can creep in at every stage of the process. It may surface as early as the decision to apply, when you weigh whether you're "good enough" to aim for a top-tier program. It can resurface when you're choosing schools or building your list, and again while preparing your application, especially if some part of your profile, such as a GPA, GMAT/GRE score, or employment history, feels weak. Even after you've submitted, self-doubt can spike as you watch others share their admissions offers or compare credentials in online spaces. (Chapter 7, The Power Shift, will say more about how you might feel after you submit.)

These feelings are not at all limited to people who typically suffer from low self-esteem. They're common even among high achievers who are used to succeeding in competitive environments. That's because the process itself invites vulnerability: You're putting yourself out there for evaluation, and it's easy to conflate admissions decisions with self-worth.

HOW TO RETAIN, OR REGAIN, YOUR CONFIDENCE

The first step in handling moments of doubt is recognizing that they're normal, even for the most capable applicants. Confidence isn't a static trait; it ebbs and flows under pressure. Rather than trying to eliminate every flicker of insecurity, focus on strategies that can help you stay grounded, regain perspective, and keep moving forward.

Normalize Vulnerability

Understand that self-doubt is a natural reaction to high-stakes evaluation. Remind yourself that your vulnerability is a sign of ambition, not inadequacy.

Remember Your Definition of Prestigious or Elite

Remember that what's considered elite or prestigious elite is relative. A program that feels like the ultimate goal for one applicant might not even register for another. Don't internalize someone else's hierarchy.

Focus on Fit over Perfection

We discussed perfectionism in the context of overcontrol; here, it's worth reiterating that admissions committees aren't looking for flawless applicants. They're assembling a class of diverse, high-potential individuals committed to personal and professional growth. Their goal is to admit a cohort of people who can learn from one another. A small weakness won't overshadow your broader story.

Manage Comparisons

Limit time spent on online forums, such as Reddit, especially if they fuel anxiety. Curate your information sources so you can focus on actionable insight rather than chatter.

Reconnect with Your Story

Revisit your achievements, leadership experiences, and motivation for pursuing an MBA. Keep a journal of compliments or acknowledgments from your performance review to revisit. Reflecting on your unique journey helps shift your focus away from numbers or competition.

PRO TIP: EVEN CEOS WERE APPLICANTS (AND INTERNS) ONCE

When you scroll through alumni success stories, it's easy to feel like everyone was born ready for the spotlight. MBA programs highlight CEOs, start-up founders, and world-changers, which can make you wonder if you belong. But every "show dog" was once a "puppy."

Take Target's new CEO, Michael Fiddelke. Before running one of the world's largest retailers, he was an MBA student at Kellogg who interned at Target. His journey wasn't instant stardom but step-by-step growth.

Admissions stories are no different. The polished bios you see are snapshots of leaders at their peak, not the anxious applicants they once were. Remembering this can help you keep perspective: You're not behind; you're at the beginning of your own trajectory.

Confidence in this process isn't about never feeling rattled; it's about having tools and the support system in place to steady yourself when you are. By resisting comparisons and reconnecting with your story, you'll find it easier to separate your worth from a single score, outcome, or comment thread. These practices not only strengthen you for admissions season but also prepare you for the inevitable ups and downs of leadership and career growth beyond business school.

Your Bottom Line

The MBA admissions journey is more than an exercise in logistics; it's a test of emotional endurance. This chapter explored the psychological side of applying: the craving for certainty, the instinct to overcontrol, and the dips in confidence that even top performers experience. These challenges are not signs of weakness; they are a natural part of pursuing something that matters deeply.

Learning to manage these emotions is as important as polishing your essays or fine-tuning your résumé. By developing emotional agility, resisting engaging in unproductive behaviors, and building perspective, you're equipping yourself not just for admissions success but for future leadership challenges that will require steadiness under pressure. Every high-stakes process, from applying to business school to pitching investors or leading a team through change, will demand these skills. This chapter is your reminder that the way you navigate this journey is part of your growth.

Next, in chapter 7, The Power Shift, we'll look at what happens after you hit submit, including both practical matters and the emotional turbulence of waiting for answers, dealing with rejection, and making decisions.

YOUR STRATEGIC SWOT

Which qualities, habits, or mindsets already help you handle uncertainty and stress effectively?

Which parts of the process bring out troubling tendencies (e.g., overthinking details, making comparisons, spiraling on Reddit threads)? How might you plan ahead to reduce these triggers or seek support? How will you intentionally counteract these tendencies to stay focused and confident?

Where could the emotional challenges of this journey sharpen the skills—such as resilience, storytelling, or decision-making—that will serve you in business school and beyond?

What support systems will you have in place to keep you moving forward during the low points of the admissions process?

How could you use feedback to strengthen your candidacy or clarify your goals?

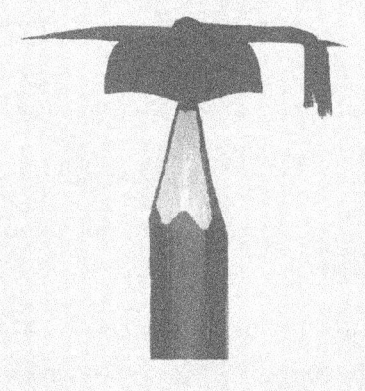

PART III

Mastering the Process

CHAPTER 7

The Power Shift

I f you've ever seen *The Lion King*, you've witnessed an example of power shifts. Young Simba is driven from his homeland after his Uncle Scar seizes the throne from Simba's father, King Mufasa. Simba eventually returns to reclaim his rightful place as king and, with the help of a wisecracking meerkat and cheerful warthog, restores balance to the land.

The MBA admissions process works in much the same way, just without the wild animals. At times, schools hold the advantage, controlling the seats, scholarships, and final decisions. At other times, applicants are the ones in charge, choosing which schools to apply to, how to frame their own stories, and which offers to accept. Understanding this ebb and flow of influence is essential, because the balance of power is never static.

Beyond the power balance between an applicant and a school, you have the added layers of power plays and power struggles within a school's ecosystem. In chapter 2, you read about profiles in power within the stakeholder web: deans seeking prestige, faculty valuing strong classroom contributors, career services prioritizing employability, alumni concerned about the reputation of their degree, and other constituencies, each with their own agendas. Schools also struggle with power imbalances between themselves and external forces, such as media rankings, market demands, and political influence.

So where does this leave you as you wait for answers from schools and make decisions about those answers? This chapter takes a look at where you do hold the power and offers strategies for managing admittances, waiting list notifications, or rejections as they come in, while building on the approaches offered in chapter 6 for managing the emotional side of it all.

The Agony of Waiting

It's not easy feeling powerless, and that's how you might feel while waiting to hear back from schools. Once your application is in, you lose direct control. You're Simba wandering across the desert. For some applicants, that lack of agency sends their stress levels through the roof and has them overanalyzing every rumor or online post as if it's a sure sign of their own fate.

It's normal to feel overwhelmed. This is a high-stakes process, and the system itself is designed to keep you on edge. Schools showcase success stories on their websites and social media feeds, the media fixates on rankings, and online forums buzz with speculation. Against that backdrop, it's easy to equate the outcome with your self-worth. So, recognizing that anxiety is built into the process is your first job. Trust that the admissions committee is doing its job: sorting through imperfect information to assemble a balanced class.

While you wait, realize that the process will move forward regardless of how often you refresh application portals. And focus on what you can control, which is preparing for the possible outcomes. Think ahead about how you'd weigh multiple offers, whether you'd reapply if needed, and what moves you might make in your career if you don't get in anywhere you want to go. By focusing on what you can control, you shift the energy from anxious waiting to strategic readiness, and that energy is your power source.

And remember, MBA programs do provide definitive answers, unlike with job applications, where candidates are often ghosted. You won't be in limbo forever.

 PRO TIP: WAIT PROACTIVELY

As you wait for answers, consider the advice of Zoe Kinias, who studied resilience while on the faculty of INSEAD: Find strength in playing out a possible negative outcome because thinking through your disappointment "steadies the anxiety of anticipation in the moment." Kinias found that "successful leaders have the capacity to anticipate and plan for setbacks, but this tactic works best 'when balanced with positivity and an ability to enjoy and experience the present moment, through optimism, mindfulness, and social support.' Being both planful and hopeful can improve wellbeing and make us more resilient if and when the worst-case scenario comes true."[62]

---

62   Amy Gallo, "How to Brace Yourself for Disappointment," *Harvard Business Review*, November 3, 2020, https://hbr.org/2020/11/how-to-brace-yourself-for-disappointment.

Strategic Moves as an Admitted Student

Getting accepted to an MBA program is kind of like being invited to a party where the host is really hoping you'll RSVP yes. Some schools won't sit back and wait for you to make a decision on your own. They will court you. For example, when Chicago Booth launched a new master's program, the admissions team didn't just send congratulatory emails. They showed up at the door of an admitted student to deliver the congratulations in person. Other schools have done the same in their own ways. Fuqua and Tuck, for example, have posted images of their admissions officers making phone calls to newly admitted students. Sure, this personal outreach is designed to celebrate *you*, but business schools have a job to do, and that is to secure a yes from you. They didn't accept you just to be nice (although they are nice!); they want you to enroll!

So, absolutely take time to celebrate in your own way, then roll up your sleeves and prepare to make strategic moves now that the power is in your hands.

 PRO TIP: ORGANIZE

When you start hearing from schools, get organized: Pay close attention to deposit deadlines, which sometimes arrive before you've heard from every school. Create a calendar to track deadlines across all your programs so you don't miss an opportunity.

MAKING YOUR DECISION: HOLDING FAST TO WHAT MATTERS MOST

It's easy to get caught up in the excitement of an offer—or multiple offers—and be swayed by factors that aren't even that important to you, especially if schools are courting you, touting all the perks and benefits of their programs. Instead, revisit the self-reflection you did in chapter 4 to remind yourself of your why for pursuing an MBA, your goals for after obtaining the degree, and the kind of environments where you thrive. What emerged as most important to you?

Remember that a higher-ranked school may not be the right choice if the financial burden feels overwhelming, the location is at odds with your lifestyle, or the culture doesn't match how you learn best. On the flip side, maybe cost is less of a constraint for you, you're geographically flexible, and all that matters is that you go to the most prestigious program. Or, you might forgo a few notches of prestige for a program that will open doors for you professionally in your preferred location. For example, I worked with a Canadian professional who was accepted at several prestigious schools in Europe but declined those offers to attend Rotman in his own home city of Toronto since that's where he wanted to work after graduation.

My point is that there is no right or wrong in terms of what your decision criteria should be. The only "right or wrong" is whether you hold on to the power that comes with knowing what you want or give the power over to others who are trying to tell you what *they* think should matter to you.

When You Have One Choice

Even if you end up with only one acceptance and rejections from every other program, you can still feel great about saying yes if that one offer checks all your boxes. If it doesn't, you can consider applying to other schools in a later round if there's still time or waiting for the next cycle to reapply to any you were rejected from.

When You Have Multiple Options

If you're fortunate enough to have multiple offers, you might have a dilemma on your hands about which one to accept. As problems go, this is a nice one to have, but it *is* a challenge. This is the time to pull out the scoring grid spreadsheet that was introduced in chapter 5. You might have used that at the beginning of the process as a way to decide which schools to apply to, and it can now be used again to decide which one to attend.

You might find that you have fresh data to add to the scoring sheet, such as how much scholarship money they're offering or a new feature of the program you learned about after starting the application process. Or you might need more information now that your tuition dollars, time, and professional future are more on the line. When you developed your list of schools to apply to, it was a wish list, and now, one of those schools is going to be your reality. So, you might want to reach out to alumni for candid conversations about your options. And be sure to check each school's recent news and social posts to see how they're evolving, and even revisit rankings if that factors into your goals. And, of course, money might tip the balance between programs, so you'll want to read the section of this chapter on negotiating the terms of an offer.

Whether you got in at only one school or everywhere you applied, hold fast to what matters to you as you venture into the "noisy room" of other people's opinions, media coverage, or any sort of buzz. For example, a client of mine applied in R3 to three schools typically ranked in the top fifteen and got accepted to all three. At the beginning of her application process, her first choice happened to be the highest ranked of the three, not just because of ranking but because it fit her criteria best. She really had her heart set on that school. But throughout the process, she'd been following WhatsApp groups for the programs and found that one of the other schools was much more active than the others, and that almost swayed her to ditch her original why and go instead with the school that had more buzz in its online forum. She was letting the noise drown out clear signals about what matters to her the most. She ended up enrolling at her original dream school.

 PRO TIP: DON'T BE A PEOPLE PLEASER

It's not that I think there's anything wrong with making other people happy, but when it comes to deciding where to go for your MBA, *you* are the only person you need to please.

NEGOTIATING ACCEPTANCE TIMING AND AID

You might be wondering if it's OK to negotiate your offer for MBA admittance just like you might negotiate a job offer—both the money involved and when your answer is expected. It is! If you're at all hesitant to do so, keep in mind that this is not the admissions office's first rodeo. Schools know that accepted students shop around. They also know that money matters. Deans often act like traveling salespeople, going around raising funds from alumni specifically to help recruit the people they most want in each admitted class. Schools compete for accepted students, and they expect some back-and-forth about scholarships or timing.

Know Your Money Objectives

Before you start negotiating the financial aspects, take a careful look at your own financial priorities and the cost of getting an MBA at each of the programs you might attend. Look beyond the headline number on a scholarship offer. The true cost of an MBA includes location and living expenses—think rent in NYC versus that in Durham, North Carolina. And don't forget how much social life and club dues can add to your budget. You might even find that a scholarship that looks big on paper might not go as far in an expensive city or at programs where international jet setting or other social travel is the norm.

 PRO TIP: BUDGET FOR SOCIAL TRAVEL

Don't underestimate how significant the social travel line item can be in your MBA budget. A recent survey of MBA students conducted through the group travel platform WeTravel Academy found that students at top US schools spend an average of $21,295 per student on social-focused group trips over the two years of their MBA programs.[63]

And once you have a picture of the true cost, bring your own priorities back into the equation, as the money factor only makes sense in the context of all the factors that are important to you. I've had clients who have turned down offers from reputable business schools with full scholarships to attend an M7 program with little to no financial aid. Conversely, a client turned down the number one

---

63   Zaky Prabowo, "3 Key Statistics About Group Travel at Top US Business Schools," WeTravel Academy, https://academy.wetravel.com/mba-travel-statistics.

ranked school in Europe to attend a top-twenty-ranked program in Los Angeles because of a better scholarship offer. It all depends on your individual circumstances. In short: Compare offers holistically, not just by the dollar figure.

 ## PRO TIP: TREAD CAREFULLY IN THE SCHOLARSHIP "ARMS RACE"

Applicants often negotiate offers using a scholarship from school A to ask school B for a match. But be aware that schools can compare notes behind the scenes. A head of admissions at an elite program once said, "We all talk. If you claim school A offered you $50,000, we'll call our colleagues at school A and confirm that before making a counteroffer." As usual, honesty is the best policy, so always negotiate in good faith.

When Timing of Schools' Responses Doesn't Line Up

When schools don't respond on the timeline you need to make a deposit or fully commit, the situation can be tricky to navigate. If you already have one or more offers but are hoping to hear from other programs, you may be able to negotiate an extension on your current deadlines. Admissions offices follow carefully planned timelines, and no amount of pressure from you is going to lead them to overhaul their process. That said, it can be worth reaching out to a school you haven't heard from, especially a top choice with a small cohort, to let them know you've received other offers.

Express appreciation for the offers and enthusiasm about the schools, but explain that you want to make the best decision and need to know all your options. Frame your message tactfully, not as an ultimatum but as a sincere expression of interest, which may prompt them to review your application sooner. This strategy works best when your current offers are from programs of similar or higher reputation than the one you're waiting on. If you're hoping for a more selective program, don't expect them to accelerate a decision, but it never hurts to ask politely.

Key Negotiating Strategies

If you decide to negotiate, whether that's asking for more time to commit or for more aid money, use common sense and context. Schools are most swayed when you have an offer from a program they consider a true peer or higher. Telling an M7 you got a full ride at a school ten spots down in the rankings likely won't move the needle, but showing them an admit (especially with aid) from another M7 might.

Market conditions matter, too. If you are reading that it's a bumper year for applications, then your A-level negotiation skills might not matter. But at other times, schools may be hungrier for a yes. I worked with a client who got accepted to an elite New York MBA program during the COVID-19 pandemic. Part of his negotiation was that he was living in New York and ready to start the program in the fall since he was not only already in the US but was local and so would not have to move during a time when geographic mobility was complicated.

Finally, know your leverage and stay professional. Approach conversations with humility and data, such as competing offers, your fit with the school's goals and values (remember that it's not all about you!), and what would make it possible for you to say yes. Finally, remember that you're pitching a future version of yourself, so you want to remind schools of how you are worth the extra investment they will make in you.

Schools expect smart candidates to ask. Just frame your request thoughtfully and be prepared to explain why an increased award or more time would help you choose them.

DECISION PARALYSIS

Ironically, one of the most stressful moments in the MBA admissions journey (after waiting for a decision) can come not with rejection but with success. Many applicants feel overwhelmed by the weight of their choices as deposit deadlines loom. Decision fatigue can set in here. Research shows that the more options we have, the harder it becomes to make a choice, and the more likely we are to second-guess ourselves.[64] After months of striving for yeses, you may feel paralyzed when you finally have to choose.

To work through this, consider the following dos and don'ts.

Don't Rush the Decision

I find myself so often needing to reassure admitted students that they will make a decision when they have to cross that bridge but that they are not yet at the bridge. So, remind yourself that if you have a deadline in a month to accept or reject an offer, you don't need to make that decision today.

Don't Rely Only on Reddit

Be careful about how much input you seek about your decision and from whom you get it. It's definitely good to have input from others, but sometimes too much is overwhelming and just leads you to feel more conflicted. Find people who truly know you and your why and

---

64   Barry Schwartz, *The Paradox of Choice: Why More Is Less* (Harper Perennial, 2004).

have your best interests at heart. That probably isn't an anonymous stranger on Reddit.

Do Trust Your Excitement

If one program excites you every time you picture yourself on campus, that's a powerful indicator. And how do you feel about the students, faculty, and administrators you've met? All that objective data you've gathered and analyzed is critically important, but not at the expense of listening to your instincts.

Do Aim for a Platform, Not Perfection

The perfect choice doesn't exist, but the right decision will be a strong platform for the next chapter of your career and life. Look at your career and education as an iterative process, which this MBA move is one key part of. If a near-perfect choice looks like it will be a strong platform for where you want to go in your professional and personal life, then that is all that matters.

Do Resist the Temptation to Compare

If you've been accepted to a school that was a reach for you but was a safety school for your friends, or if you got into one in the lower rungs of the top ten but everyone else is boasting about their HSW acceptances, try not to get caught up in the comparison game. If you are pleased with where you're going, that's all that matters.

The Sting of Rejection

No matter how accomplished or confident you are, hearing no can feel like a judgment on your worth as a person. When a school says no, or even wait-lists you, it's natural to take the decision personally. But admissions decisions are not indictments or perfect reflections of merit. They are outcomes made by a committee balancing institutional priorities you can't control: class composition, industry balance, timing, or other priorities. A no can simply mean you weren't the best fit right now, not that you're lacking potential or promise or won't ever get accepted to that school or others.

If you still feel strongly about the school that rejected you, map out a reapplication strategy. Or you might choose to pull yourself up from the disappointment of rejection to use it as a catalyst to pursue other programs that weren't on your original list. I've seen applicants be rejected from schools, only to apply and get accepted to programs with even stronger reputations or better fit the next go-round. That was the case with an applicant in the aerospace sector who made it to the interview stage but ultimately didn't get into an M7 school that was his first choice. After the rejection came, he thought he'd just apply again the next year, but I encouraged him to apply to some other schools in R3. He ended up receiving two acceptances, including to another M7 school, which he accepted and found was an even better fit for him.

Analyze your application to determine what could have been stronger and start addressing those areas early. Consider retaking a test, adding quantitative coursework, or gaining more leadership experience. Get outside input on your essays. For example, I worked with someone who was rejected after working with another consultant. I reviewed the essays he had written in his application and observed that there were tons of "I" statements. That was a red flag because it failed to show that he would be a team player! We replaced many of the "I" statements with "we," and he ended up getting accepted to Columbia Business School.

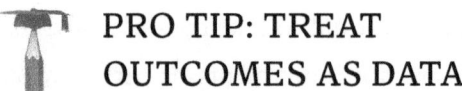

PRO TIP: TREAT OUTCOMES AS DATA

When you treat each application outcome as data to inform your next move, you regain some of your power.

HOW TO BOUNCE BACK FROM REJECTION

Rejection hurts, but it doesn't have to define your future. The key is not to eliminate disappointment but to channel it productively. The strategies below will help you process the emotional sting, regain perspective, and turn this chapter of the MBA journey into a stepping stone rather than a stumbling block.

Embrace a Growth Mindset

Research shows that high performers thrive when they view setbacks as opportunities to grow rather than proof of fixed ability.[65] Adopting this mindset allows you to see rejection as part of the process of becoming stronger, clearer, and more competitive.

Reframe "Failure" as Feedback

Rejection isn't proof you're not talented. It's data about how you presented yourself, about your timing, or about a school's needs. Use it as insight. I've seen many applicants leverage one year's no into the next year's yes by applying what they learned. Schools do not see reapplication as a black eye but as a positive sign of your resilience.

---

65   Carol S. Dweck, *Mindset: The New Psychology of Success* (Random House, 2016).

Allow Yourself to Pause

It's OK to take time to process disappointment. Give yourself permission to "hibernate" for a few days before reengaging with next steps. Emotional recovery is part of resilience.

Look for Ways to Connect

Research in social psychology has shown that, "as social animals, we need to feel wanted and valued by the various social groups with which we are affiliated. Rejection destabilizes our *need to belong*, leaving us feeling unsettled and socially untethered."[66] So, if you experience a sense of loss or feel off-kilter in some way after a business school rejection, look for ways to get involved with friends, family, or colleagues to regain your sense of connection.

Find the Hidden Value in the Process

Even if you don't get the outcome you hoped for, applying to business school is an investment in yourself. You emerge with a polished résumé, a stronger personal narrative, and a deeper understanding of your goals and your worth. Also, the application journey itself can be a networking opportunity that can open new doors through the many people you meet along the way. Kyla Sherap, a member of the Ross class of 2027, expresses this well: "The MBA application process was a lot of dedicated self-exploration into what I value, what kind of person I want to be, and how that translates into my career goals."[67]

---

66   Guy Winch, "Why Rejection Hurts So Much—and What to Do About It," TED, December 8, 2015, https://ideas.ted.com/why-rejection-hurts-so-much-and-what-to-do-about-it/.

67   "Ambition in Action: Meet the Michigan Ross Full-Time MBA Class of 2027," Michigan Ross, October 20, 2025, https://michiganross.umich.edu/news/ambition-action-meet-michigan-ross-full-time-mba-class-2027.

Put Rejection in Perspective

The admissions process is imperfect, and many admissions officers will admit to that. Committees juggle countless factors, and outcomes don't always match talent or effort. Recognize that another candidate's acceptance doesn't make them better. Timing, institutional strategy, and unseen considerations all play roles.

PRO TIP: DON'T FORGET THAT ADMISSIONS REPS ARE ONLY HUMAN

A former assistant dean at an M7 school once shared that a deserving applicant was denied admission multiple times before being accepted to the program. With so many factors making the process imperfect, this can happen often, and admissions folks and deans wonder what kept them from accepting those superstars in the first place!

BUILD MENTAL AGILITY AND EMOTIONAL ENDURANCE

The leadership development and organizational change professor at INSEAD, Manfred F. R. Kets de Vries, declares, "Disappointment is not meant to destroy us. If taken in stride, it can strengthen us and make us better. In spite of its devastating emotional impact, we may even consider encounters with disappointment as journeys toward greater insight and wisdom."[68]

---

68   Manfred F. R. Kets de Vries, "Dealing with Disappointment," *Harvard Business Review*, August 22, 2018, https://hbr.org/2018/08/dealing-with-disappointment.

I encourage you to think of rejection as a training ground for resilience. Learning to stay grounded under pressure is a leadership skill. There will inevitably be more disappointment coming your way in your career—the promotion you don't get, the pitch that doesn't result in a deal—so think of application rejection as a "boot camp" training you for that!

Cognitive reframing techniques borrowed from cognitive behavioral therapy can help build mental agility. For example, instead of interpreting rejection as a signal to panic, see it as proof that you're challenging yourself.

These strategies aren't about erasing disappointment but about transforming it into momentum. Rejection and disappointment are part of any career journey. By embracing a growth mindset, reframing setbacks as opportunities, and giving yourself permission to regroup, you'll approach future challenges with more confidence and strategic clarity, whether in a future admissions cycle, a career pivot, or a boardroom negotiation.

 ## PRO TIP: OUTLAST "NO"

"Sometimes, it takes hearing 'no' a hundred times before one 'yes' changes your life. To anyone out there doubting themselves: Keep going. You're closer than you think." This advice comes from HBS MBA student Radha Kamdar, who was told by someone, "You'd be better off buying a Louis Vuitton bag" than trying to get into business school. But she went for the designer MBA instead of the designer purse and gained admission to the full-time MBA at Harvard.[69]

---

69   Radha Kamdar, "You'd Be Better Off Buying a Louis Vuitton Bag," LinkedIn, accessed October 15, 2025, https://www.linkedin.com/posts/radha-kamdar-016295194_youd-be-better-off-buying-a-louis-vuitton-activity-7366313763400040449-2j0a.

Acing the Waiting List Game

A decision to wait-list can feel like a rejection, but it isn't. Disappointment is natural, but being wait-listed is actually a form of good news because it means you're still in the running. Schools use the waiting list to manage class size and yield. The best strategy is to follow each school's specific guidance for what to do while on their waiting list.

Some explicitly invite you to update them; others prefer minimal communication. Only send meaningful updates that add new information (for example, a promotion, a new project, or an improved test score). Resist the urge to flood the admissions office with extra recommendations, lengthy letters, or gifts. Those rarely help and can actually hurt. Instead, focus your energy on strengthening your position for the next round or cycle in case you need to reapply to the same school or apply to additional schools.

 PRO TIP: ALIGN FOLLOW-UP WITH A PROGRAM'S VALUES

One past client of mine was placed on the waiting list at an elite full-time MBA program. Rather than waiting passively or following up in the same way most wait-listed applicants would (e.g., sending an update on their latest projects at work), I encouraged him to be creatively strategic in his approach. This program happened to use a particularly unique essay prompt in their applications. So, I encouraged him to submit a waiting list update using the same innovative format as the essay prompt. By doing so, he stood out from other applicants who most likely submitted the typical waiting list letter and gave another proof point of his alignment with the personality of the program. He got in!

Your Bottom Line

Waiting for decisions can feel like circling in a holding pattern waiting for your plane to land, but you do have power in how you deliberately make your decision and prepare for every possible outcome. There is also power in remembering that you *will* get an answer.

Once the yes arrives, keep in mind that schools will pursue you because they want your enrollment as much as you want their seat. Your challenge is to resist the noise—programs courting you, rankings boasts, friends' opinions, online chatter—and return to what you clarified in chapter 4 about your values, goals, and fit. And remember that schools will not be surprised if you try to negotiate the timing of your commitment or aid money they are offering. Just realize that admissions offices are not all-powerful.

Power in admissions isn't about controlling the process; it's about knowing when to act strategically, when to step back, and how to hold fast to your own priorities.

YOUR STRATEGIC SWOT

Where are you most vulnerable to pressure—friends' opinions, rankings, or decision fatigue—and how can you keep those from overriding your own decision criteria?

How can you turn this stage into an advantage through building relationships with additional students and alumni at your targeted schools, clarifying financial priorities, or using a rejection as the start of a reapplication strategy?

What external factors (timing mismatches, social media comparison, unexpected waiting list outcomes) could cloud your judgment, and how will you safeguard against them so that your final choice reflects your goals rather than outside noise?

Which qualities or circumstances give you leverage as an admitted student—scholarship offers, admits at comparable programs, or a compelling fit with your top choice—and how will you use them to negotiate tactfully?

CHAPTER 8

Making the Most of Your MBA Experience

W hether you were admitted on the first try to your dream school, spent months navigating waiting lists, or had to reapply in a later round or a whole new cycle, you've reached the finish line. You're in! So, take a victory lap and celebrate the results of your hard work. You've earned a seat in the classroom, and now what you do with it—how you approach academics, engage with classmates, and position yourself for career opportunities—will determine the true return on your MBA investment.

 PRO TIP: THERE'S ALWAYS NEXT TIME

If you didn't get in this time, try not to despair. You can try again. Meanwhile, you might find the "Co-Create Your Professional Experience" section of this chapter helpful as you develop a plan B. And this whole chapter will help you get a jumpstart for when you do start an MBA program!

As you think about that MBA return on investment (ROI), keep one word in mind: *co-creation*.

The term *co-creation* was coined by Michigan Ross marketing professor Venkat Ramaswamy and described later in the *Harvard Business Review* as "about putting the human experience at the center of the enterprise's design ... in which individuals are invited to influence the future of enterprises in partnership with management."[70] For example, when LEGO released a Sonic the Hedgehog set, the plastic bricks version of the spiky blue speedster wasn't created by the company's own designers but from a submission made by a twenty-four-year-old fan in the UK.

 ## PRO TIP: CO-CREATION AS ATTITUDE

While co-creation involves taking action, it starts with a mindset. As NYU Stern's Vice Dean Nate Pettit puts it, "You can't control every outcome over the next two years, but you can control your attitude ... [and] attitude is the single best predictor of how much you'll grow here and how well you'll carry that growth forward."[71]

Columbia University has applied this concept in an application essay prompt they've used, which essentially asks applicants how they

---

70   Venkat Ramaswamy and Francis Gouillart, "Building the Co-Creative Enterprise," *Harvard Business Review*, October 2010, https://hbr.org/2010/10/building-the-co-creative-enterprise.

71   Nate Pettit, "Consider Being a 'Contributor' During Your Time as a Student," NYU Stern MBA Admissions, July 17, 2025, https://wp.nyu.edu/stern_full_time_mba/2025/07/17/consider-being-a-contributor-during-your-time-as-a-student/.

will put themselves at the center of their own experience design and, in turn, influence the business school and the MBA program.

"We believe Columbia Business School is a special place with a collaborative learning environment in which students feel a sense of belonging, agency, and partnership—academically, culturally, and professionally. How would you co-create your optimal MBA experience at CBS? Please be specific. (250 words)"[72]

Whether or not you applied to Columbia in a cycle that included the co-creation prompt, I encourage you to reflect on it now, because your MBA is only a launchpad for what comes next. To make the most of the experience, don't just show up and assume everything will fall into place. You'll need to co-create your experience on three fronts: academic, social, and professional. These are what make your MBA more than just a credential.

Co-Create Your Academic Experience

You can shape what you get out of the classroom by the choices you make in courses, projects, and faculty engagement. Let's take a deeper dive.

MAKE ROOM FOR BOTH EXPERIMENTATION AND INTENTIONALITY

Co-creating your academic experience means balancing experimentation with purposeful crafting. Of course you want to be mindful of your professional goals; however, playing it safe by signing up only for classes you're confident you'll ace or sticking to subjects that perfectly match your career goals may give you a strong transcript

---

72   "MBA Application Requirements," Columbia Business School, https://academics. business.columbia.edu/admissions/mba/application-requirements.

and résumé but not necessarily the growth that future employers (and you) will value. In chapter 7, we talked about the concept of growth mindset—pushing yourself in areas where you feel least confident, learning from mistakes, and seeing setbacks as part of the process. The same applies here.

That might mean enrolling in a quant-heavy finance course if your background is in communications or taking a leadership lab that puts you on the spot in front of peers when you'd normally avoid the spotlight. It might mean spending your summer at an early-stage start-up where the paycheck is modest and the outcome uncertain, but the lessons in grit, adaptability, and resourcefulness will stay with you. Or it could mean joining a global case competition where you're suddenly immersed in a problem space far outside your expertise.

In his "8 Lessons I Learned as a First-Year MBA Student," Daniel Gberbie, Duke Fuqua class of 2026, captures the balancing act of experimentation and intentionality powerfully: "Unless your career path demands it or being on the Dean's list is a personal goal, the true value of this experience is what you take from it, not just what grade you earn."[73] He encourages creating a list of skills and knowledge areas you want to strengthen and then being intentional about enrolling in courses that fill those gaps.

CURATE YOUR LEARNING PORTFOLIO

Your mix of classes and other academic experiences is like an investment portfolio. With both, you want to be strategic and selective and always build toward your goals. When choosing your concentration,

---

73   Daniel Gberbie, "8 Lessons I Learned as a First-Year MBA Student," *Duke Daytime MBA Student Blog*, September 8, 2025, https://blogs.fuqua.duke.edu/duke-mba/2025/09/08/daniel-gberbie/8-lessons-i-learned-as-a-first-year-mba-student.

elective courses, and other opportunities, such as optional certificates or experiential learning, strike a balance between what you want—your subject matter interests and career goals—and what the job market wants, such as particular skills, knowledge, and experience. In today's digital economy, that likely means a course in AI or data science.

 ## PRO TIP: BE A T-SHAPED LEARNER

Workplaces value people who combine breadth and depth in their knowledge and skills. The T-shaped model, originally developed and used internally at McKinsey & Company in the 1980s, describes someone with deep expertise in one area (the vertical bar of the T) and broad fluency across other domains (the horizontal bar of the T). Variations such as H-shaped and π-shaped have cropped up, but no matter what you call it, the model serves as a reminder to resist the temptation to stay rigidly in one lane. Choose electives and experiments that stretch you while developing ever-deeper competency in your core skill sets and subject matter knowledge.

RELATIONSHIPS ARE THE REAL CURRICULUM

The network you build while in business school and the things you learn about yourself as you interact with people during your program may not end up as grades on your transcript, but these are key parts of the curriculum. If you treat study groups, team projects, and classroom debates as competitions or just as tasks to survive, you'll miss out.

One graduate of Michigan Ross shared one of her biggest regrets during the MBA: "I wish I had been more intentional about building deeper relationships with classmates I didn't work with on teams. Between work, school, and family, it was easy to default to the people I knew best."[74]

These experiences are chances to iron out the kinks in your leadership, communication, and teamwork style while expanding your worldview as you work and learn with classmates from a variety of cultures, life experiences, and work styles. The classmates you connect with in these settings may become future business partners, or at least people who will pick up your call when you need a sounding board as your career progresses. Also, professors aren't just grade-givers; they can become mentors and collaborators long after you graduate.

INTEGRATE, REFLECT, AND SUSTAIN YOURSELF

It is all too easy to fall into the trap of sprinting from class to recruiting event to group meeting without stopping to connect the dots. Real learning happens when you integrate. Take time to journal, reflect, or simply walk and think about how the ideas from your finance course intersect with your digital strategy course and with the innovation lessons from your team project. Remember why you came to business school in the first place and consider whether your academic choices are helping you honor that why.

Thriving academically depends on wellness, balance, mental resilience, and sometimes knowing when to call it a night. It can also mean saying no and not trying to do or be part of everything. An LBS grad has this advice: "There is so much to do that it's impossible

---

74   Jeff Schmitt, "2025 Best & Brightest Executive MBA: Cathy Taylor, University of Michigan (Ross)," *Poets & Quants for Executives,* August 6, 2025, https://poetsandquantsforexecs.com/students/2025-best-brightest-executive-mba-cathy-taylor-university-of-michigan-ross/.

to do everything, so choose what you want to do and commit to it …
Embrace the fear of missing out. It is an inevitability."[75]

Co-Create Your Social Experience

The admissions office of your school has vetted thousands of applicants to build an incoming class of some of the most interesting and ambitious people you might ever meet. You may never again have the kind of access you get during your MBA to such a wide range of people from dozens of countries and industries you've only read about, and with personal stories that will inspire you. Admissions did the prework for you; now, it's up to you to make the most of this curated network of highfliers!

You will shape not just your social experience now but also your friendships and professional network for years to come. Some students *really* take this advice to heart and even find a marriage partner![76,77] Finding wedded bliss might not be on your MBA bucket list, but there are plenty of opportunities for platonic friendship-building and socializing that the following approaches can facilitate.

GO BEYOND THE SMALL TALK

Even though your MBA classmates are some of the most interesting people you will ever meet, it's surprisingly easy to skim the surface of

75   Robbie Laing, "10 Things I Learnt from My MBA Experience," *Student and Admissions Blog, London Business School*, July 18, 2022, https://admissionsblog.london.edu/10-things-i-learnt-from-my-mba-experience/.

76   Marco De Novellis, "From MBA Classmates to Soulmates: How Business School Couples Found Love," *BusinessBecause*, February 14, 2024, https://www.businessbecause.com/news/mba-degree/9205/business-school-couples.

77   Jenn Yee, "Why the Odds Are Good for Finding a Husband or Wife at Business School," *Manhattan Prep*, May 12, 2011, https://www.manhattanprep.com/gmat/blog/why-the-odds-are-good-for-finding-a-husband-or-wife-at-business-school/.

those relationships, just sitting together in class, grabbing quick coffee chats, and keeping things polite but shallow. The real opportunity is to go deeper.

One alumna spoke of this powerfully: "My entire Booth experience is built on the foundation of strong friendships, both male and female. While I cherish every connection at Booth, I am especially grateful for the friendships with other women who have helped me navigate big personal, professional and academic moments. From discussing fertility to full time job offers to Financial Statement Analysis, these relationships are the best ROI I could have asked for."[78]

MIX VERTICALS, INDUSTRIES, AND CULTURES

You may feel an immediate pull to the classmates who share your professional background—consultants with consultants, bankers with bankers. But if you only stick to the familiar, you'll miss the cross-pollination that makes business school such a unique experience. Be deliberate about reaching across divides. Join a student club that lets you explore emerging interests. You come from a tropical climate? What about the ski club?! Sign up for a cultural night hosted by classmates from a different part of the world. Go to a case competition in an industry you know nothing about. Stretching yourself socially is part of your overall educational experience.

A recent Tuck alumnus had this advice on that subject: "Get involved in everything you can … Try something you haven't tried before … Growth happens at the edge of your comfort zone."[79]

---

78 Mac Witmer, "The Power of Female Friendships During the MBA," *The Booth Experience* (blog), May 26, 2022, https://theboothexp.com/2022/05/the-power-of-female-friendships-during-the-mba/.

79 "Fred Kamuzinzi T'25," Tuck, https://tuck.dartmouth.edu/pathways/fred-kamuzinzi.

PRO TIP: THINK BEYOND
YOUR CAMPUS

Your MBA network doesn't stop at the edge of your own program. Take advantage of student club events with peer schools, and meet other MBA students at conferences and treks and through social travel. Just as you would never limit your network to people at your own company when out in the world, don't limit it now to one school.

SEE TRAVEL AND TREKS AS RELATIONSHIP ACCELERATORS

Social travel is one of the defining elements of MBA life (and sometimes costly, as I talked about in chapter 7). You might get to know your classmates while snorkeling the coral reefs of Fiji amid colorful parrotfish and giant clams and sipping piña coladas on the beach or when skiing the French Alps on a visit to your classmate's winter chalet during a holiday break.

Whether it's exotic travel halfway around the world or an industry trek to Silicon Valley, these shared adventures create bonds that classroom time and months of casual coffee chats can't replicate. That doesn't mean you have to say yes to everything. Your bank account and your energy will thank you for being selective. But recognize that these shared journeys are part of the MBA's hidden curriculum.

Co-Create Your Professional Experience

An MBA accelerates your professional advancement not just because the degree itself is an automatic ticket to bigger and better opportunities, but because the experience enhances your skill sets, subject matter knowledge, and professional network. Plus, it's a chance to gain greater self-awareness and confidence around your strengths and to polish your professional presence. When you approach your professional experience during the MBA intentionally and strategically—when you co-create it—all this is possible.

Sounds exciting, right? But then, you might scroll through Reddit and see these sorts of posts:

- "I graduated from a top 10 MBA program in May (not M7). Now it's September and I'm still unemployed. I've applied to 300+ roles ... Got 20+ interviews ... but none converted into offers."

- "I was there too this time last year, only I was from HSW ... Problem with 1000 applications and only 3 offers at the end ... is having to stomach almost 1000 rejections. That wasn't fun."

- "I went through the same job search process. It's all luck really. I too applied to over 500 jobs."

With comments like those, you might think I've lost my mind when I suggest that you co-create your professional experience in your MBA program, particularly around your postgrad job prospects. Can you make a difference if it's really just all about luck? Absolutely! Sure, there's always an element of serendipity in a job search. But there are aspects of the process you *can* control, starting from the moment you begin your program until the day you walk at your graduation ceremony and beyond. Let's look at some high-level strategies that enable you to do so.

FIND THE UPSIDE

Despite being a rough year for the job market, the 2025 GMAC *Corporate Recruiters Survey* found that 99 percent of global employers expressed confidence in business schools' ability to prepare graduates for success within their organizations, and one-third expected to increase their hiring of MBA degree holders over the prior year.[80] Whether the job market you graduate into is tight or the demand for MBA grads outpaces supply, try to find the bright, hopeful spots. The GMAC statistic was brought to life when I met Sundar Pichai, CEO of Google with an MBA from the Wharton School, who reassuringly addressed the issue of the 2025 job market by saying, "We're always looking for great talent."

In most years, it's common to see MBA placement rates (the percentage of students with job offers three months after graduation) at over 90 percent. And in years with tough job markets, the rates are still in the 70- to 80-something percentage brackets.[81] When you see profiles of elite MBA grads with the "open to work" banner in LinkedIn, try not to be alarmed. First off, the placement rates three months out are never 100 percent (though some schools come pretty close, such as the University of Georgia Terry College of Business's

---

80 *Corporate Recruiters Survey: Dean's Summary,* GMAC, 2025, 1, https://www.gmac. com/-/media/files/gmac/research/employment-outlook/2025-corporate-recruiters- survey/deans-summary.pdf?rev=4e12e661fc764934a230f3353fe3465f.

81 Marc Ethier, "Data Dive: 2024 MBA Salaries, Bonuses & Job Placement Rates at 30 Top-Ranked B-Schools," *Poets & Quants,* March 21, 2025, https://poetsandquants. com/2025/03/21/data-dive-2024-mba-salaries-bonuses-job-placement-rates- at-30-top-ranked-b-schools/.

recent banner year of 94.7 percent![82]), so there are always going to be some grads who don't land quickly. Plus, some newly minted MBAs might be deep in start-up mode, seeking capital, building their teams, or refining their business plans, so they're not counted as "placed," even though they're fully engaged in their ventures. Others may have received job offers but are holding out for a better fit or negotiating for timing, location, or role. And keep in mind that life happens and takes people off course, so some grads' job searches are delayed by illness, a family issue requiring their attention, or choosing to take time off to travel.

The key is to stay positive, remembering that you have grown your network considerably in ways you probably could not, or would not, have done without going through an MBA program. So make the most of that wider network. That network includes anyone who has helped you in your MBA journey, even your admissions consultant, if you worked with one. For example, since I have a robust network of MBA alums on LinkedIn, I have made introductions for current (and even prospective!) students, as well as alumni, to support their career advancement efforts.

BALANCE CLARITY WITH EXPLORATION

With the investment of time, money, and effort you put into your MBA, you can't afford to drift aimlessly when it comes to career goals. At the same time, this is one of the few moments in life when you can try out new paths with relatively low risk. The challenge is to strike the right balance: Get clear enough early on so you're not dabbling

---

82   Cole Claybourn, "15 MBA Programs with the Most Employed Graduates," slideshow, August 29, 2025, https://www.usnews.com/education/best-graduate-schools/slideshows/mba-programs-with-the-most-employed-graduates?slide=14.

without direction, but leave room to explore options you might never have considered.

Has anything changed about your short-term or long-term professional goals from the application phase? Once you've considered that, sketch a career horizon with the roles, industries, sectors, and locations that genuinely spark your interest. If your focus could use some work, make use of resources your career center is likely to offer, such as career assessments, alumni panels, and facilitation of informational interviews. Then, give yourself permission to test career alternatives through electives, club involvement, or short projects, as well as through the more obvious option of internships.

At no other time will so much attention be given to strengthening, building and expanding one's career prospects than during the MBA educational journey. That's why I'd encourage every MBA student to network as much as possible and to maximize utilization of the resources and services offered by their MBA career office.

—PEDRO GONZALEZ, PRESIDENT AND FOUNDER
OF TALENTMBA, WHICH CONNECTS MBA
STUDENTS TO VENTURE CAPITAL, PRIVATE
EQUITY, AND START-UP OPPORTUNITIES

The key is to avoid being so rigid that you miss out on discoveries or so scattered that you leave with no clear path. Aim for achievable targets in the first three to five years post-MBA, while keeping alive a broader, more aspirational trajectory for a decade or more out, which is likely to include some experimentation and risk-taking.

SYNCHRONIZE YOUR BRAND, STORY, AND NARRATIVE

Remember that businesspeople are bombarded with emails all day, pulled into countless decisions and meetings, and tethered to their phones. They're also likely to be interrupted every two minutes during core work hours, according to Microsoft's Work Trend Index,[83] so, if you're going to be the cause of one of those interruptions as you network and job search, you have to make it worth their time. Having a clear professional narrative that relays the core of your brand cuts down on the mental energy and time others have to spend trying to figure out who you are, what you need, and how you can help them or others they might connect you with. The advice around crafting your story for your application in chapter 4, and the emphasis on consistency across elements of your application in chapter 5, still applies. But now, instead of résumés and interviews to get in, you're focusing on résumés and interviews to get out!

As you work toward your professional goals, you'll have networking conversations, summer internship and post-MBA job interviews, and opportunities to make yourself visible with extracurricular leadership and social media posts, especially on LinkedIn. Throughout all that, what you've done before, what you're doing now during your MBA program, and what you want to do after all need to present a consistent personal brand.

So, make sure that the elevator pitch you use to introduce yourself to new connections, plus your résumé bullet points, LinkedIn updates, and cover letters, all reinforce each other. Employers and even savvy networking contacts will notice if the dots don't connect, so make sure everything you put out there tells the story you want to tell.

---

83 "Breaking Down the Infinite Workday," Microsoft, June 17, 2025, https://www.microsoft.com/en-us/worklab/work-trend-index/breaking-down-infinite-workday.

PRO TIP: USE THE RESOURCES AVAILABLE TO YOU

For more on the fine points of career planning, job search, and career management, I recommend taking advantage of all the resources in your business school's career center and these books:

- *Designing Your Work Life* by Bill Burnett and Dave Evans (Vintage, 2021)
  This book uses approaches out of Stanford's "D School" design thinking lab to identify your best-fit career options.
- *Give and Take* by Adam Grant (Penguin, 2014)
  Wharton professor and host of the acclaimed podcast *WorkLife*, Adam Grant explores how our interactions with others shape our success.
- *Job Moves* by Ethan Bernstein, Michael B. Horn, and Bob Moesta (Harper Business, 2024)
  This team of authors from the faculties of HBS and Kellogg encourages you to think of each job as a platform for progress. Learn to "interview the job" instead of just being interviewed.
- *Navigating Your Next* by Julian Lighton (Advantage, 2026)
  This former McKinsey consultant and chief strategy officer at billion-dollar tech companies offers a pragmatic and comprehensive approach that balances strategic insights with granular tips to help elite professionals figure out what they want—their "next"—and get it.
- *Working Identity* by Herminia Ibarra (Harvard Business Review Press, 2023)

- LBS professor Ibarra presents novel approaches to career reinvention, including experimentation, accepting that a career is not a linear path, and new approaches to networking.

BUILDING YOUR NETWORK CAPITAL

As the saying goes, "Your network is your net worth."[84] Your MBA years are a great time to start building that "net worth," or adding to the networking capital you've already begun accumulating in your career so far. Networking isn't just about uncovering job leads or getting your résumé to the top of the pile. It's about developing a circle of peers, mentors, and future collaborators who will be far more to you (and you to them) than distant LinkedIn connections. A full exploration of networking strategy could fill another book, but the high-level principles that follow, combined with the tips offered earlier in this chapter about co-creating your social experience, will help you approach networking with purpose, authenticity, and long-term vision.

 PRO TIP: NETWORK WITH ALUMNI BEFORE YOU ARE ONE

Learn from the hindsight of this UNC Kenan-Flagler alum, who said, "Looking back, I wish I had started reaching out to alumni much earlier in my MBA journey. I began connecting with them primarily when it was time to start recruiting for healthcare roles

---

84 Several books use the title *Your Network Is Your Net Worth*, but the original published use of the term is believed to be the book *Your Network Is Your Net Worth: Unlock the Hidden Power of Connections for Wealth, Success, and Happiness in the Digital Age* by Porter Gale (Atria Books, 2013).

... Engaging with alumni earlier would have given me a clearer understanding of the healthcare recruiting process, the nuances of different career paths, and how to best position myself for success ... While I eventually found my footing, having that early guidance would have made ... the job search even smoother."[85]

Go for Network Breadth and Depth

Remember the idea of a T-shaped academic experience? The same can apply to your network. Go deep by aiming for a core group of colleagues who will form the inner circle of your network. These are the folks you can turn to for just about anything, and they know that you'll do the same for them. But it's not realistic to think you're going to be that close with the hundreds or thousands of people who will make up your network, so also look for breadth—of industries, functional roles, locations, ages, career levels, and more.

Optimize Your Network Beyond Your School

Also network with other programs, such as the executive MBA or part-time MBA, or with students and alumni of other schools within your university outside of the business school. Even consider networking with undergrads. Remember, there are many influential alumni from a university's undergraduate program. One of my clients at USC Marshall praised the caliber of the broader USC network. It was also interesting to learn that USC undergrads who went to other business schools, including HBS and Booth, came back to their undergraduate alma mater to recruit MBA students.

---

85   Jeff Schmitt, "2025 MBA to Watch: Uriah Ford, North Carolina (Kenan-Flagler)," *Poets & Quants*, August 19, 2025, https://poetsandquants. com/2025/08/19/2025-mba-to-watch-uriah-ford-north-carolina-kenan-flagler/.

This might mean putting yourself out there, like a member of Yale SOM's class of 2026 who organized a meetup in Los Angeles for media and entertainment interns across different business schools to which more than one hundred students showed up.[86] This is the kind of creative thinking that top business schools, such as SOM, value in applicants as they assess how you will contribute to the community— co-creation in action, or that "contributor" attitude described earlier.

Make Networking a Two-Way Street

Networking works best when it's reciprocal. It's not just about collecting contacts or asking for help; it is also about contributing value to others. Be sure to offer introductions, share information or resources, and take a genuine interest in the goals of people you meet. When you approach networking as a mutual exchange rather than a transaction, relationships deepen and trust builds. Over time, that generosity tends to come full circle, often when you least expect it.

PRO TIP: RESPECT THEIR TIME AND MAKE IT WORTH THEIR WHILE

When reaching out for a coffee chat or Zoom conversation, conventional wisdom says to ask for just fifteen minutes, but for many busy professionals, that can still feel like a big ask. Before you hit "send," think about their perspective. What might make the conversation worthwhile for them? Maybe you share a professional interest, want to discuss something they've written, or

---

86 "Internship Spotlight: Nico Sahi '26, Illumination Entertainment," Yale School of Management, July 16, 2025, https://som.yale.edu/story/2025/internship-spotlight-nico-sahi-26-illumination-entertainment.

volunteer with a cause they support. A quick online search can reveal small breadcrumbs of common ground. When you show that you've done your homework and that the exchange could be mutually valuable, you're far more likely to get a yes and to start the relationship on the right note.

Network Even When You're Remote

If you're completing your MBA entirely or partially online, you may find it harder to build a network, but you can, as long as you're intentional about it. In addition to the more obvious avenues of LinkedIn connections and getting to know your professors, don't forget about classmates. Just because you aren't striking up impromptu conversations sitting next to each other in class doesn't mean you can't develop into professional colleagues. Instead of passively attending virtual classes, ask thoughtful questions to make yourself visible, and follow up with other students outside of class.

Online programs work hard to ensure you don't miss out on the relationship-building side of the MBA experience. At UNC Kenan-Flagler, students meet in person at quarterly "Summits" in cities around the world and on the Chapel Hill campus, where they collaborate on projects, attend workshops, and strengthen their professional bonds. In Rice University's online MBA, students tap into a global alumni network and regional chapters that organize in-person meetups and mentorship opportunities, blending the flexibility of remote study with the community of a traditional MBA.

Play the Long Game

The connections you make in business school may help you find your first post-MBA role, but their real value often unfolds over years or even decades. Networking isn't something you build once and check off your list—it's a lifelong investment. Just as you were encouraged earlier in this chapter to think about both your short- and long-term career goals, apply that same mindset to your network. Focus on relationships you can nurture over time, not just ones that serve your immediate job search.

Michigan Ross explains the long game this way: "When you go forth as an alum … You'll have a natural network there because our alumni are helping one another. Even when they're 50 years old and thinking about a career switch or moving to a different company, they're reaching out to a fellow alum to pick their brain. This support does last a lifetime."[87] If you're pursuing your MBA in your twenties or thirties, the networking needs you'll have decades from now might not seem very pressing, but if you build a strong network early in your career, particularly with your program's alumni of all ages and career stages, you will thank yourself when that day comes!

PRACTICE CAREER AGILITY AND RESILIENCE

Job searching can feel like the ultimate test of your patience threshold. No matter how strategically and authentically you network, clarify your goals, and curate experiences that position you as a strong candidate for your post-MBA career, you may still find yourself frustrated when you take that show on the road to land a postgrad position.

---

87   Wendy Correll, quoted in "Michigan Ross Alumni Network: Lifelong Career Support," University of Michigan Ross School of Business, https://michiganross.umich.edu/alumni.

The mindset to adopt is the same one we discussed for rejections or waiting lists during the application phase: agility, reflection, and growth. You'll also no doubt have to practice those things during your MBA program, but this can feel incredibly hard when you feel more like a passenger on a plane flying through turbulence than a seasoned pilot. This was the experience of one HBS alum who first stepped on campus with the goal of soaring into a leadership position in the travel industry. Then COVID-19 hit. He ended up having to go to plan B—returning to his former consulting firm, where he racked up more valuable experience and was ultimately able to make his desired career move after the travel sector bounced back. His advice to others? "Following your dreams can be turbulent; bumps requiring course corrections can come without warning. It requires looking up and taking a leap of faith that things can work out."[88]

 ## PRO TIP: ALL THAT GLITTERS IS NOT CAREER GOLD

A close friend I made during a semester exchange at Wellesley College (I was there from Vassar; she was from Middlebury) graduated from Yale SOM in the 1990s and rose to a VP position at the world's third-largest asset manager in Boston but stepped down the ladder to a lower-level position that she enjoyed more. Try not to chase titles or marquee brands at the expense of fit. Culture, the people you will work with, and the day-to-day work matter most. If a move aligns better with your values and strengths, it is a step forward, even if the title suggests otherwise.

---

88   "Ryan Flamerich (MBA 2021)," Harvard Business School, accessed October 6, 2025, https://www.hbs.edu/mba/student-life/ryan-flamerich.

Agility and resilience can also mean having backup options and using them wisely. That might mean broadening your search to a different functional role, shifting industries, relocating to a different city or country, further training to expand your tool kit of in-demand skills, or taking on contract or interim work while continuing your search. Alumni and career offices can also help connect you to smaller firms or start-ups that may not recruit on campus but can offer hands-on experience and rapid paths to higher levels of responsibility. The key is to stay visible and engaged rather than withdrawing out of frustration or embarrassment.

Also, remember what I've said about how the career stories you see featured on business school websites and alumni blogs are carefully curated. Schools highlight the standout successes—graduates with impressive titles and rapid promotions or who support a particular mission of the school—not the full range of experiences. Plenty of MBA grads take longer to find the right fit, or they shift directions entirely. That's why it's so valuable to talk with current students and recent alumni who can give you a more realistic, behind-the-scenes view.

 ## PRO TIP: PURPOSE COMES IN MANY FORMS

Not everyone is destined to go into impact investing, and that's OK. Many business schools focus on broader social impact professions, so you might find that grads working in those areas will dominate speaker panels and alumni profiles. But the world also needs great product managers in consumer good companies that produce everyday essentials, from breakfast cereal to Band-Aids. The work you do doesn't have to sound world-changing to be meaningful. Whether you're advancing the infrastructure in an emerging market or in charge of property expansion at Marriott, you're contributing to something bigger than yourself. And remember that when a former Stanford MBA goes on to become prime minister of the UK, that may make global media headlines for obvious reasons, but it doesn't make your own impact any less valuable. Also, think about this point that a client who is a second-year MBA student shared with me: "The true meaningful opportunities are not always in the big-name brand firms, they are working for the more successful individuals."

The career search during an MBA can feel at times like a boot camp in bouncing back, resetting, and moving forward. If you can co-create your professional experience with that mindset, you'll leave school not just with a degree but with the adaptability that defines great leaders.

 ## PRO TIP: SIT, STAY, ... NEGOTIATE?

Co-creating your MBA experience to develop valuable skills isn't just for your postgrad career. The benefits can show up in unexpected ways. A Berkeley Haas alumnus found that his sharpened negotiation skills paid off at home: He and his wife moved from a three-year stalemate about what type of dog to get to a one-week consensus—settling on a European Doberman![89]

---

89   Susan Petty, "A Competitor Relishes Collaboration and the Berkeley Haas Culture," *Berkeley MBA* (blog), February 20, 2025, https://blogs.haas.berkeley.edu/the-berkeley-mba/a-competitor-relishes-collaboration-and-the-berkeley-haas-culture.

Your Bottom Line

Making the most of your MBA is an exercise in co-creation: You design your academic path, your social fabric, and your professional runway.

Start with experimentation that stretches you, not just classes you'll ace, and build a T-shaped profile that balances depth with breadth. Curate an academic portfolio that mixes theory and practice.

Treat classmates and faculty as part of the learning itself—relationships as curriculum. Integrate and reflect so the dots connect, and protect your energy (the world won't come to an end if you say no to some social invitations, trips, or clubs!).

On the professional side, balance clarity with exploration: Define a primary goal, test one or two secondary paths, and keep your story, brand, and choices aligned.

Network for now and for later, practicing reciprocity and widening your circle across schools, locations, and formats.

Finally, plan for agility: Job markets shift, three-month stats don't tell the whole story, and detours can accelerate your career if you stay visible, persistent, and resilient.

YOUR STRATEGIC SWOT

Identify the academic strengths and curiosities you can deepen now, the stretch areas you're willing to tackle, and the habits (reflection, wellness, time management) that help you learn fast and recover quickly.

Note any gaps that could limit you, such as not enough networking or a tendency to overload and burn out.

Select electives, labs, and projects that build marketable skills while broadening your perspective; use treks, conferences, alumni outreach, cross-school clubs, and online touchpoints to expand your network; line up "secondary experiments" (short projects, internships, contract work) that can lead to unexpected opportunities.

Anticipate external factors such as tough job markets, visa or geopolitical constraints, financial limits, or FOMO that dilutes your focus, and counter them with contingency plans. Those might be alternate roles, industries, locations, or interim work.

CONCLUSION

The title of this book, *It's Not About You*, has always been a little tongue-in-cheek. Of course, in many ways, MBA admissions *is* about you. You are the one navigating applications, offers, waiting lists, and—heaven forbid—rejections. You are the one with ambitious goals, loads of potential, and a unique story to tell. But as I set out to write this book, and to give it a name, I thought about the golden threads throughout all the support I've provided to clients over the years in response to their questions and concerns, and those threads led me to the title.

One of those threads is that you, the applicant, are one element in a complex, dynamic, and sometimes baffling system in which a web of stakeholders, a host of micro and macro influencing factors, and a hefty dose of serendipity are at play. So, no, it's not really all about you!

Another thread is the power of strategic storytelling to persuade that system that you are right for their program. Sure, you're the main character in your story—the hero, even! —but experiences you choose to write about in essays, highlight on your résumé, and talk about in interviews are as much about the system as about you. Your story must speak directly to the needs and agendas of admissions committees and all the stakeholders in the MBA web as they construct an incoming class. So, once again, your fingerprint is all over your application, but it's not only about you.

And, finally, I wanted to take the *you* out of the emotionally challenging parts of the MBA application journey. I don't pretend to be a therapist, but I wanted to give you a clear window into the psychology of applying to MBA programs. If parts of the process rattle you, you're not alone, as even ordinarily confident, accomplished professionals experience doubts about their candidacy (Am I good enough? Am I M7-worthy?). That's why I devoted a full chapter to the psychology of applications and tried to weave throughout the book a steady acknowledgment that the ups and downs are normal, nothing to be ashamed of, and absolutely manageable with the right tools. By recognizing that you are not the only rider on the emotional roller coaster, and by seeking support through the resources I've talked about, you can shift from anxious you to the comfort of we.

Nine Truths of MBA Admissions

Across all the strategies and tips I've shared with you are some fundamental truths I'd like to leave you with. Think of this as a sort of executive briefing on key points to keep in mind.

1. B-schools don't admit applications. Humans admit humans.

   Behind every portal update is a committee of people sipping Diet Cokes, managing timelines, and debating differing opinions. *Your* job is to make *their* job easier: Tell a clear story, connect the dots for them, and make your value easy to see without sending them on a scavenger hunt across résumés, essays, and recommendations. Tell them who you are as a whole person, and remember that they are people, too.

2. In the absence of facts, don't fall into the trap of assuming the worst.

   The application process has natural quiet stretches. When silence extends, your brain will try to fill the blanks. Don't let it. Create routines that keep you grounded, invest in relationships, and limit the doomscrolling. When in doubt, return to your narrative and your why. Clarity is the antidote to anxiety.

3. Admissions officers are portfolio managers.

   They're assembling a cohort of students who can learn from one another and meet institutional goals. Your task is to show how you add distinctive value to that mix, whether from your industry perspective, resilience, creativity, or leadership on real projects. If you are admitted, it's because they can picture you strengthening the portfolio. If you aren't, that may say less about you than about this year's portfolio needs.

4. Risk management plays a role in decision-making.

   Business schools are in the business of educating and mentoring leaders and changemakers. Notice I said, "in the business of." Good businesses have to manage and mitigate risk. You can't solve for every variable they are trying to control, but you can lower perceived risk by being consistent across application materials, showing self-awareness about your gaps, and offering evidence (not empty adjectives) that you are who they need. If you're choosing among offers, remember you do risk management too: Map your goals against each program's setting, support, and opportunities, *not* against anyone else's excitement.

5. The value you bring > the value you take away.

    An MBA isn't only about what you'll gain; it's about what your classmates and the school as a whole will gain because you're there. That mindset shift changes how you interview, how you contact alumni, and how you show up in admitted-student channels. And if you don't get the answer you hoped for, keep the same mindset. Continue building relationships with the people you met along the way, from admissions officers to current students and other applicants. There's real ROI in those connections, regardless of the outcome.

6. Stories influence more than statistics.

    Your story is the through line that makes your choices make sense: why you want this degree, why now, and why there. If you have to reapply, collect new evidence that advances your narrative, such as stretch assignments, leadership moments, community impact, and clearer goals. If you're matriculating, your story becomes the foundation for internships and the postgrad job search.

7. Don't expect the experts to agree.

    Even within one committee, perspectives differ. Across schools, they diverge a lot. Even we admissions consultants don't always agree. That's OK. Filter the noise through your values and good judgment. Seek counsel, absolutely, but know that you own your final decisions about where to apply, when and how to apply, and how to present yourself. You're designing a path that fits you, not following an exact science.

8. Persuasion beats perfectionism.

Perfect essays don't exist. And even if they did, they alone wouldn't guarantee admission. What does exist is a persuasive, consistent case for fit and contribution. As you move into next steps, keep asking, Am I making it easy to understand who I am and how I'll show up? That applies to scholarship appeals, admitted-student surveys, reapplication plans—everything. Aim for clarity, not over-the-top prose, and prioritize impact over perfect polish.

9. The past doesn't have to predict the future.

If you didn't go Ivy League as an undergrad, that doesn't mean you're shut out of top MBA programs. You're not the same person you were at eighteen—you've built new skills and delivered real results, and you have a new story to tell. So don't get stuck in "I'm not [fill in the blank with your dream business school] material." Similarly, if a test score is less than you hoped for or a detour in life has stalled your professional path, let that disruption be a vehicle for demonstrating better self-knowledge, a stronger professional narrative, and the confidence to advocate for yourself. And if you didn't get the admit this time, lace your boots back up and try again, or take the outcome as a signal to pivot—maybe to a new role or industry.

You've Got This

Thank you for letting me sit beside you in these pages during a season of your life that might be simultaneously exciting, stressful, and hope filled. I wrote this book to narrow the distance between applicants and the realities of admissions, to make the process feel less like a mystery and more like a set of choices you can own.

Wherever you're headed next—into an MBA program, onto a reapplication plan, or toward a career role that suddenly feels more possible because you did this hard thinking—I'm cheering you on.

By even considering going for an MBA, you've already demonstrated the two qualities that travel well in any environment: intention and courage. Keep both close and good things will come.

ACKNOWLEDGMENTS

This book wouldn't be possible, in all sorts of ways, without the support of my husband, John Hibel. Although he came close to getting his MBA in the 1990s, with applications started for Darden, Kellogg, and Tuck, he ended up working on the corporate audit staff at General Electric in the Jack Welch era, which was its own form of top-notch business education. (He also took the first year of MBA courses at Sloan during his undergraduate education at MIT.)

I would also like to acknowledge my sons, Christopher Coward and Matthew Coward, who have taught me the importance of pursuing your passion, whether that is flying an ERJ145 at eighteen thousand feet for a regional airliner or initiating a meeting with a retired US Navy admiral to explore a future in public policy.

My brother, Reverand Dr. Robert Melhorn, has shown me the importance of ministering to others as an adult (and how to catapult oyster crackers into New England clam chowder as a child!).

I wouldn't be the genuine and conscientious professional I am today without the example of my parents, who passed away in

February 2020 and October 2024. Not a day goes by that I don't think about them.

A heartfelt shout-out to my best friend, Liz Sohn, whom I met during college breaks working at Harvard University forty years ago. With one brother at Harvard Law School and another at Harvard Medical School at the time, she introduced me to the elite world of graduate education—and its legendary campus parties. Her boundless kindness defines true friendship.

The world of admissions consulting thrives on collaboration, and I'm grateful for the kindness and support from amazing peers such as Andrea, Hillary, Marlena, Menette, Nupur, and Scott. I've learned so much from each of you.

My prior role consulting with business schools elevated clients to lifelong friends, including Dee, Jennifer, Kathy, Signe, and Zack. They proved that some of the finest admissions professionals can be found at state universities.

Finally, I would like to thank the entire Forbes/Advantage team who made this whole experience seamless and enjoyable. In particular, I simply couldn't have done it without my collaborative editor, Michelle, who is truly one of the most impressive professionals I've met in my entire four-decade career.

ABOUT THE AUTHOR

Barbara Coward is a globally acclaimed authority in MBA admissions, respected for her unparalleled strategic approach to one of the most competitive admissions processes in higher education. With more than twenty-five years' experience on both sides of the admissions desk in the US and abroad, and having earned an MBA herself, Barbara's insider perspective has resulted in her clients on six continents gaining acceptance to the world's most selective business schools.

Barbara established one of the UK's first professional MBA admissions offices and later served as a marketing consultant for domestic and international business schools. In 2016, she founded her consulting practice, MBA 360 Admissions, recognized in *Poets & Quants* in 2024 for a "Perfect 10" client satisfaction score in its ranking of admissions consultants. Known for her expertise in strategic storytelling and applicant positioning, Barbara mentors clients to present their strongest case for admission. Her clients have been admitted to Stanford Business School, Harvard Business School, the Wharton School, and programs in London, Paris, Munich, Barcelona, Toronto, Hong Kong, Singapore, Dubai, and beyond.

Barbara is frequently sought out by major media outlets, including Bloomberg, *Fortune*, *Financial Times*, *Poets & Quants*, *Business Insider*, *Money*, and *US News & World Report*, for her insights into the evolving MBA landscape.

A graduate of Vassar College, Barbara began her career in corporate finance in Boston and London for global brands, including American Express and Laura Ashley.

www.ingramcontent.com/pod-product-compliance
Lightning Source LLC
La Vergne TN
LVHW050942210226
832072LV00002B/5